The funniest joke about modern world: Its free and open !

(Or) Was modern world able to retain intact, the Enlightenment era values of uninhibited human-liberty and freedom?

(Part-11 in the series : Is modern democracy a fake-coin? Part-1 is available at Amazon.com link:
http://www.amazon.com/modern-democracy-fake-Reinvented-ebook/dp/B008NNPG32/ref=sr_1_2_title_0_main?s=books&ie=U)

Author: Abraham J. Palakudy

An independent philosophy, Reason, mind and polity researcher,
and, founder of the philosophical research oriented non-profit organization, 'Conscience of the society'

Our web-site: www.conscienceofthesociety.com

Our other book: 'Is reason a sense-organ? A super-mind above the known mind ?' (Amazon.com link:
http://www.amazon.com/dp/B008NOEE9I)

Introduction to part-11 of the book

Part one of the series, which was published during 2012, (Is modern democracy a fake-coin?) was more on the question as to why a *reinvented democracy* was a pressing need of our age.

This part-11, though overall related to the same theme, ie. around the need of a 'reinvented-democracy', delve deeply on the never-noticed evil features of modern democratic world, such as the **free-market** idea almost replacing the notion of uninhibited, plain, existential freedom of man. (article-1)

Modern world, especially the Western-world, do not at all accept any other notion of human-freedom than that propagated by the industry, ie. the notion of freedom represented by the FREE-MARKET ideologists ! This is one of the major reasons why modern world has failed to retain the real 'enlightenment-era' spirit of the idea of the 'rights, equality and freedom of man', held to be self-evident, and endowed by their Creator as unalienable'.

Unfortunately, a small percentage of men in the post-industrialized world, who could thrive on their unbound free-spirit and creativity, found the new world, including the new political institution that turned around them, bestowing in their hands a complete mastery of the world ! What clicked was the huge-accumulation of capital in their hands, the new deciding factor of real Power in the new world ! The universal notion of human-freedom, individual dignity and liberty, the exclusive gift of history to mankind had, thus, died down in the cross of the new 'capitalized' world.

Article-2 on the fate of 'Liberalism' supplements whatever has been discussed in article-1, ie. the sad culmination of the notion and idea of European Liberalism into a kind of society that article-1 has described.

Article-3 handles the psychology of 'one-up-man-ship' syndrome, a common feature of modern democratic-capitalistic world. More than an urge to improve the quality and quantity of one's material consumption, or various gadget-based conveniences of life, what modern man aspires in the modern-world is a constant stepping-up on the ladder of 'success', wherein 'success' has been defined, and set more on one's social status and relevance.

Article-4 shifts the gear into an altogether different area of modern life, the sphere of wide-spread violence that she encounters every day at every corner of the world, either by the regular menace of *terrorism,* or by the inter-community attempt to destroy the other community, and have exclusive control over society, modern-states' ever-increasing acts of atrocities on single-citizens or upon their organized groups of dissidents, and finally, that between single man-to- man ruthless acts of violence ! The article attempts to arrive at a base-classification of all violence into TWO universal types, so-that mankind could have a better understanding of this 'self-annihilating' tendency of our species.

Articles 5,6 and 7 are similar to the 10 such articles listed in part-1 of this series, ie. describing why a *'reinvented democracy'* a must for mankind.

Article -8 expresses the net crux of what is ultimately wrong with modern word; it throws clear light onto the evil of the 'means' (modern states) usurping the real ' end' of the state, as well that of every other institution in the world- the individual citizen ! The primordial evil myth and superstitions around a RULER and a 'state' play havoc with modern life on planet-earth, causing many of its serious conflicts, wars and internal-uprisings.

Article-9 show-cases why modern world is NOT an open, progressive and modern place on earth, but a continuation of the dungeon of the old 'rightists' way of social, economic and political hegemony in society.

Article-10 reiterates the idea that article-3 has handled. It shows how modern world desire, and hence intentionally create an 'un-equal' society. It is a deliberate endeavor, hence, her superficial sermons on the need of an 'equal-world' is a big lie, and a blatant self-deception.

The last article, article -11 offers the solution ! If a reinvented democracy could usher-in a better world, upon what all values and laws that it could be built-in ? What should an ideal democracy represent to people and humanity ?

The biggest joke that the inhabitants of modern-world believe-in is that, or what they are forced to believe by the current-masters of the world is that, it is a FREE and OPEN world ! Its freedom is very peculiar. For an example, in many Indian States in her North-Eastern region, a particular special law called 'Armed Forces Special Power Act' (AFSPA) is prevalent for many years, to curtail the anti-state insurgency of militant groups within the these states. A lady activist, Irom Charu Sharmila was on hunger-strike from 2000, and it still continuing ! She is kept under home arrest by the State for the crime of 'attempt to suicide', and she is force-fed by the state through nasal tubes ever-since. State is unmoved, despite her 15 years of protest !

The power to protest and dissent makes no sense when the State is a typical Power-State, where allowing uninhibited freedom to people is just anathema and blasphemy when looked at from the point-of view of her Power-State angle ! Hence, calling our age free and open is just blasphemy, and a great joke ! There is nothing to support the claim that the age is free, except its false freedom to express dissent to a certain degree. As well evident from all the articles listed in the book, it is plainly clear that, humankind is in dire need of a paradigm shift with regard to her idea of FREEDOM, man to man, and state to man relation. Human Reason gets stagnated when it is not free, and what modern world suffers most from is a permanently suspended state of rationality.

Index

Article-1

Is Free-market a guarantee for free-society ?

(Or) Can the basics of human freedom and FREE-MARKET concepts one and the same thing?)

(The following link leads to a very inspiring speech by a teen-age girl at a UN conference, giving simple directions as to what the political, social and intellectual institutions of the world should adopt to usher a better world !:
https://www.facebook.com/video.php?v=852988084731533)

We, the freedom crazy men of contemporary world, would never imagine that the very concept of **human-freedom** also can have fake models !

It seems that for the Western world, basic concept of 'human freedom' is almost one and the same with Free-market concept !

It is a very deep and serious philosophical issue today, especially when the very institution that is supposed to 'represent' people, (democratic governments) is dangerously conflated with the 'free-market' forces. This situation marks the virtual absence of a '*conscience*', or a **rational center** in the modern world.

This writer encountered the stark reality of the above, from an encounter with a reputed 'freedom' organization recently, and this is an attempt to throw light on this serious issue, for the serious attention of every one who cares, and uphold the pure concept of human-freedom !

He (the writer of this post) used to be in the mailing list of a reputed West-based, international *freedom* organization for quite sometime. They recently announced a formal membership drive, for the sake of like minded men and organizations to join them, for sharing innovative freedom ideas. When our organization was filling-up the on-line questionnaire for registration, the first item baffled us:

' What attracted you to the FREE-MARKET idea ?'

Was the base concept of human-freedom nothing but the 'free-market' ideology for them? Free-market in the sense that, the freedom of the entrepreneurs class to do business under the legendary 'laissez-faire' policy of governments

Our organization was, in-principle, against the modern tendency of world's more than 55% of the wealth and resources getting increasingly accumulated in the hands of, as few as 70 or 80 rich business families and corporate-entities, as recently found by reputed research bodies such as Zurich University and Oxfam. So, we were not attracted to the unconditional 'free-market' idea. Therefore, after filling-up the form for membership with the above stand, nothing was heard about our membership !
For a typical westerner, any reference against 'free-market' is judged as a leftist, or socialist or pure communist bent of mind. Or in other words, an enemy of the freedom of individual. There is no other model, unfortunately, is alive or known today in the contemporary world, wherein basic freedom and dignity of individual citizens are treated separately from the free-market concept.

Now the crucial question is; would a society bent-upon 'free-market notions, simultaneously be a society that seriously care for human-freedom in its traditional and philosophical sense too ? Or, at least the way it was most profoundly expressed in the Declaration of American independence; " that all men are created equal, that they are endowed by their Creator with certain unalienable Rights, that among these are Life, Liberty and the pursuit of Happiness " ?

Ayn-Rand was very sharp to detect this subtle, but very specific difference between the two kinds of freedom models. She states that there was a very specific shift from the original *political rights* to *economic rights,* in the later years of American democratic development. In her words;

" the gimmick" was the switch of the concept of rights from the political to the economic realm....the democratic party platform of 1960 summarizes the *switch* boldly and explicitly; ' will reaffirm the *economic bill of rights* (such as right to job,income, home, health, education etc.) which Franklin Roosevelt wrote into our national conscience sixteen years ago' (her book, ' Capitalism, an unknown ideal')

Ayn Rand, though she was radical capitalist, and wrote all the above in her frustration and great anger against 'state-control', her anguish against pure rights and freedom of citizens (including that of entrepreneurs !) must be taken in the right spirit. She took every citizen as a model entrepreneur !

The real 'globalization' of industry started with its real reign over the political freedom of common man happened after her death in early 1980,s. So, she was probably not aware of the usual perils of the excessive influence of the industry in the later-stage world, wherein every government collaborating with it, for maximum so called 'development' of the world.

Erich Fromm, though her contemporary, was more aware of the perils of the excessively aggressive industry, over the rights and freedom of ordinary men. He writes;
" ..while the canalizing of all human energy into work and the striving for success was one of the indispensable conditions of the enormous achievements of modern capitalism, a stage has been reached where the problem of *production* has been virtually solved and where the problem of the *organization* of social life has become the paramount task of mankind' (his essay ' selfishness, self-love and self-interest')

Probably because of the intensity of the 'cold-war experience, the West seem to have developed a kind of 'paranoia' about protecting entrepreneural freedom, out of her fear for state control over the free-market model.

Today, being those who talk about the world in *first-person are* the industry in the contemporary world through the *media* that they predominantly own and run, the **FREEDOM** they talk about is exclusively their freedom, the freedom of the entrepreneurs, and the market, their own realm selling their finished products and services !

They virtually are the world; its exclusive activity, and the content in the modern day ! Everything rest in the world is the 'means' for their primary existence, and for their professional activity ! Concept of human race outside their institutional perspective is an illusion, and a great void ! World in its essence, is a great market-place , and human life is a matter of unending needs, and their professional activity of meeting these needs. Any talk of individual freedom etc. outside the perspective of the above realm of economic activity is sheer blasphemy for the above contemporary owners of modern world! That is why every institution that stands for FREEDOM in modern world is organizations that stand for *free-market,* founded, funded, and run by and for them ! Leading industrial nations boycott other nations when the latter do not participate in the *free-market* operations, **Grave issues of abuse of human rights and freedom of such nations are matters of secondary concern.** As far as markets are open, such political entities are considered free and open ! Matters of right and freedom abuse would be considered as their 'internal' concern !

As a result of the above narrated **free-market obsession** of modern world, grave abuses of individual dignity, rights and freedom by political regimes are routine and rampant. Rights and freedom of Individual citizens are either grossly neglected and despised by the totalitarian political regimes, or by the so called 'democratic-capitalistic regimes. While in the first model above, if the citizens are mere passive commodity for the primary existence and relevance of the state, in the second model, they are same kind of commodity for the flourishment of the *free-market* based industrial activities. While China is the prime example of the first model, USA and other advanced industrial nations are examples of the 2nd model.

Though USA champions itself as the role model of human freedom in the entire world, its disturbing features such as her having the maximum number of prisoners in the world, and frequent human-rights violation incidents (like the recent shooting of a black-teen by police, and the 'choke-holding' and killing of another black-citizen) dampen the authenticity of such claims. The recent 'OCCUPY wall-street' type agitations in US, wherein the citizens raised spirited slogans that, 99% of the population is under the reign of 1% elites, she exemplified the reality of the 2nd model above. It is the reign of the 'free-market', and not the reign of the kind of freedom the founding fathers of USA had envisioned.

In countries like India, who scramble to claim the rank of a fast developing economic super-power, citizens' grievances and genuine representations never reach their destination in various government offices and ministries ! They are despised and ignored at the corridors of power, and their representations routinely find their place in rubbish-bins. Their so called political freedom is confined only to their right of having routine work-strikes, and the mass-protest assembling in cities and villages, seeking various rights and privileges, giving the impression to the world that, citizens are free and empowered! An unattached single citizen is the most helpless and powerless entity in modern democratic-capitalistic society, thus leaving the very concept of FREEDOM a myth! Then, what to talk about the freedom of him in the so called 'free-market' economies?

India's present central government(from 2014 ...) is all set to launch a massive 'development' agenda for the country, without first attending to the primary need of providing ordinary citizens his deserving dignity in the street, at home and at various citizen-government meeting points. Most of the democratic constitutions in the world has specific directives to ensure 'DIGNITY OF INDIVIDUAL' (fraternity clause in the Indian constitution) in the governance delivery system.

Without first strictly adhering to the above central and primary guideline of country constitutions, simply collaborating with the industry for 'development' will only damage the very fabric of human freedom, dignity of individual and the progress of human civilization. The quality of life of individuals will not ever naturally improve merely with his quality of life in the *quantitative sense*, ie. **making available abundant supply of life-amenities in the market !** The ever-present profit motive in the *free-market* system will contribute to making these life-amenities (even quality food and homes !) increasingly un-affordable to large section of the population, thus leading to serious social unrest. So, there is an urgent need to understand and treat 'freedom' and 'free-market' concepts differently and separately.

Susan George, a fiery activist against new-liberalism said:

"Business and the market have their place, but this place cannot occupy the entire sphere of human existence" (In her paper presented at 'Conference on Economic Sovereignty in a Globalising World'

Bangkok, 24-26 March 1999,see
link: file:///C:/Documents%20and%20Settings/Father/Desktop/A%20Short%20Histor
y%20of%20Neo-liberalism%20%20%20Global%20Exchange.html)

Article-2

Where has LIBERALISM landed us ?

Why a universal value of 'striving for success' not a sustainable model for healthy societies?

It is a sad fact of the modern world that, the ideal of the celebrated European Liberalism has ended-up in a rat-race for individual success, whether it is in its direct field of commercial-entrepreneurship, political power-market, academic competition for upper-hand in the knowledge market, or in the simple social-leadership field.

If you wish to have FREEDOM from not to be bothered by others, or from not coming under their freedom -disturbing use of the will, or that of their collective institutions like governments, one need to isolate himself from such realms of life and society, that he can afford to be **independent of others,** and the whims of their above said collective institutions. For gaining such independence from others and their collective institutions, one simply has to rise above every one in 'success' in whatever field he is in. At such levels of material or conceptual success, he **definitely gains freedom** of the kind that he has been seeking. At such levels of success, he could interact at an equal footing with other equally successful men, and at the same time, stands escaped from the acts of judgment and botheration of the ordinary folks and their collective institutions !

It is impossible for someone dependent on some others, to be free by any standard. His freedom would be conditional to the wishes, likes and dislikes of such others whom he is depended upon, for leading his life ! **In this sense, some degree of success was an inevitable feature of the liberal principles of old Europe.**

Let us listen to what Paul Verhaeghe, senior professor at Ghent University, who holds the chair of the department for psychoanalysis and counseling psychology says :

"Our presumed freedom is tied to one central condition: we must be successful – that is, "make" something of ourselves"
(Ref'
link: http://www.theguardian.com/commentisfree/2014/sep/29/neoliberalism-economic-system-ethics-personality-psychopathicsthic)

Or, if you want to be free without the above condition of success, you could do so by abandoning not only sucess, but also the very kind of society that keeps those standards; the Hippie movement of 1960's was such an attempt to have freedom without being a part of the above rat-race; these men and women made a failed attempt to be 'free', by abandoning the very society that insisted on certain 'standards' to be one among them.

From the above seen pre-condition of 'success' behind the tenets of European Liberalism and its singular goal of 'freedom' of the individual, it becomes obvious that it was the Liberalistic tendencies that had paved way for modern capitalism. Free-market has become synonymous with 'freedom' in the European world ! When the community or the State 'leaves alone' the entrepreneur, for his fullest expression of the creative wealth-creating acumen, such community or country started gaining the reputation of being a 'free-society'. Of course, this model of economy, society and polity had paid its fruits of plentifulness to Europe: wealth had poured in abundance into that region of the world !

Such States and communities that put restrictions on national and international free-trade have been accused to be 'closed-markets', with 'socialistic' tendencies. Concept of Freedom started gaining its symbol and meaning exclusively on the basis of the freedom of its entrepreneurs. Universal freedom of human-being as an essential political and metaphysical element has lost its centrality from the modern world, and from the prime-priority status of political establishments, in an extremely unfortunate turn-out !

Sociologist Zygmunt Bauman neatly summarized the paradox of our era as: "Never have we been so free. Never have we felt so powerless."

Not only powerless, but people are also get accused (especially the ones who could not make it to the top) that they were 'losers and scroungers"

Prof. Paul Verhaeghe continues in his article referred above:

"We are forever told that we are freer to choose the course of our lives than ever before, but the freedom to choose outside the success narrative is limited. Furthermore, those who fail are deemed to be losers or scroungers"

In a social and economic struggle by every one to become successful, it would end-up in a logically inevitable mathematical pattern : in the strict hierarchical order such growth takes place, no two persons can be at the same slot of the chain of success. One always has to be in a bottom number from the other ! This series of successful men should inevitably leave a lengthy bottom tail of unsuccessful men too, or those who could just make it NOT to get extinct from the race to survive ! Every authentic research outcome shows that, this hierarchy-line is getting thicker and thicker at the top-stretch, leaving the bottom part of the line thinner and thinner, in an increasingly distinct and clear pattern! These studies and statistics shows that more than 55% of the wealth and resources of modern world is snow-balled into the hands of the top 1% (or even less than 1% ?) most successful, or say, the most FREE men ! Or in other words, as in USA's OCCUPATION agitators allege, modern world is the reign of 1% over the rest 99% !

The slots of Freedom are open to everyone, but unfortunately, the very system of Liberalism lets only the ones at the top of the hierarchy to be more free than the ones at the bottom.

What liberalism had at bottom aspired and stood-for, has lost its element and purpose in the modern world.

Article-3

Seeking origin of the notion of human 'success', and up-man-ship values

The existence of a realm other than the physical, where the conceptual 'self' of man reside is an irrefutable reality. If the 'body-man' reside at the pure physical realm of the world, the social-entity (the ego) of man reside in the conceptual realm. Besides the food, sex and safe-stay needs of the physical man, human-being also needs an 'exaltation' of his person-hood.

Besides his physical body and face, he also sees in the mirror a parallel self, his face and expression as he is seen and accepted in the society. He is the real entity that lives his life, unlike our counter-parts in the animal kingdom, who live only their physical lives.

The mirror image is his 'objective' identity that others see in the world ! World here is a market-place where all these multitudes of 'objective' human-beings dwell. Others not only see his physical body and features, but also his personality, ie. what he is in society. Though this 'spirit' (in the sense that, this aspect of the self is an intangible energy)does not need food, water etc for its survival, it can not survive without its conceptual, or say, psychological needs, that is, constant reiteration from others in the form of acceptance, approval, or some or other kind of behaviour in responses to its own behaviour ! Such responses are the vital evidence and reiteration that, he is real and socially alive !

'Success' is a 'halo' that every-human-being desires to wear around him in society. Society judge him on the existing criteria of 'success' prevalent in each society.

Modern man, unfortunately, due to strongly prevailing myths and norms around 'success' and up-man-ship in the world, always want to become someone-else; he always feel incomplete about himself as he is !He always tend to feel that, what is more real about life is somewhere upward in the success-ladder of society.

Criteria of assessing this 'success' differed from age to age. Remember, success is after all the ' halo' with which man desires 'others', or the world that constitutes this others, remember him with, during and after his life ! In the older days of frequent physical confrontations, smart warrior-ship' was one of those conceptual halo with which every one wanted to survive with in the present and future conceptual world. When Kings replaced the super-warriors in history, he himself wore the halo of the most-successful, the most feared and revered. The most exalted dream of each child of those ages was his/her becoming a King or Queen one day! As only one could become a King or Queen at any given time, the rest defined their success by becoming someone close to the King and Queen.

The way King walked, talked, dressed and behaved had become the ultimate reference point of quality behaviour and quality life. Though, no one might have dared to emulate him openly, at least in the dreams of all men, that was the pinnacle of everyone's imaginable success !

The ones who were in the King's list of favorites had become Feudal Lords, or huge-estate owners. If not like Kings, these Lords also had developed their-own styles of dress, food-habits, behaviour and values of their-own as days passed. Though the basic food stuff they ate and the base-raw material for the dress they wore too were same, the stuff they made with those raw-materials were quite different from that of common human-beings. They were eager to mark their different class, by differentiating their style from that of the ordinary class of people. The actual difference in the degree or power and freedom (both are always interwoven in every society, at every age !) they enjoyed in society was thus established by displaying such difference in the way of life and style.

These higher class of men spent large amount of resources/money to ensure this distinction of their class up and above from that of ordinary folks, thus making it impossible for the latter class to emulate their ways, or prohibit them by way of the restrictive cost-factor ! The real pleasure these fortunate men and women enjoyed was not the higher taste-value of the food they ate, or the value of the dress and other bodily accessories they wore, but the actual higher class distinction they had in society. Their men and women always attempted to emulate the style and tastes of the King himself, as they were the highest model for emulating !

History says, the concept of Gentlemen was thus born in Europe by cementing such traditions of dressing, foot-wear, facial-hair style, behaviour and language style etc. by these class of King's secondary line of Knightly and Lordly men and their families.

The story after the Industrial revolution

The concept of 'success' and up-man-ship had acquired a firm institutional form since the industrial revolution. European Liberalism's most conspicuous outcome was the origin of capitalistic tradition in the world. Capitalism celebrated whatever was most prized about liberalism, the unfettered human-spirit of freedom and creativity. The new class of entrepreneurs were left free to do whatever they want to improve their lives !Men and nations fiercely competed each other for up-man-ship in industry and trade.

Industry had thrown-open a world of unnamed Royalty and Knight-hood before the new entrepreneur-class. They were able to possess everything that the then Feudal-Lords used to have in the society; big mansions, servants and even bigger capital-reserves. It is heard that many a Knights of the day in Europe were willing to exchange their Knight-hood in exchange of the exotic items these new industrial class had brought from strange foreign-lands !

Rule of Kings had ended, and the power and relevance of the old Feudal Lords also has subsided considerably. Industry sector has side-lined the old agriculture-centered growth and economy. The new world had bestowed nations in the hands of the new entrepreneur class, in a dramatic shift of power and glory from the old Royals and Feudal Lords!

These new class of entrepreneurs had taken-away the mandatory blue-blood requirement to become a Lord or Noble of material success. These new men of vast-richness might-have taken all the care to adopt the ways of the Lords and Nobles with regard to their dressing style, foot-wear standards, food habits, language and behavior norms, in-order NOT to look different from them in any degree or manner ! The class of 'Gentlemen' had arisen in Europe during this period; David Cody, Associate Professor of English, Hartwick College, in his paper 'Gentlemen' says:

"Members of the British aristocracy were gentlemen by right of birth (although it was also emphasized, paradoxically enough, that birth alone could not make a man a gentleman), while the new industrial and mercantile elites, in the face of opposition from the aristocracy, inevitably attempted to have themselves designated as gentlemen as a natural consequence of their growing wealth and influence"

Here we directly encounter the delicate theme of this paper; ie. the concept of 'success' had been always one class' attempt to migrate into the fold of the next upper-class ! More than amassing adequate wealth for his family and his future generations to come, the chief goal attained by the neo-rich of the industrial revolution era was the uplift-ment of their class to an already existing, well recognized higher class in the society. While his actual quantitative value of wealth was confined to his own personal knowledge, his occupying a palace equal in size and pomp as that of the Nobles of the time, and his dressing like him and eating, behaving and speaking like them had transformed him and his generations to the Noble class in letter and spirit ! His kin had also internalized the ways of such upper class. Therefore, 'success' was in reality, a migration into a higher- plane of life, exemplified by clear, tangible symbols.

The economic development that followed the industrialization era was remarkable in creating different levels, or planes of social-relevance hierarchy in the world, each such level was marked or symbolized by the use or possession of certain degree of luxury dwelling units, passenger vehicles, the total value of properties and assets owned, the value and style of apparels and foot-wear they have worn, the way each class spoke, and kind of their food-style, and the quality and expensiveness of house-hold articles at their homes !

Restricting one's ambition to any certain degree or level has started to be considered a draw-back or short-coming of the values these new Lords were expected to keep. Success was a limitless going-up on the ladder. There were enough and more ready-made planes or class-distinctions in the new-world, for every such ambitious men to reach and roost. Each such higher class clearly distinguished the class-difference instantly, by the above symbols and signs each member exhibited.

An exclusive political system was built-around such economic difference in the modern society that, it measured and defined the 'progress' of their respective nations on the basis of the 'success' of these entrepreneurs. The base model of States and nations that shined in Europe and USA had become empirical example of the success of such model of growth and progress, for the entire world.

Progress of nations has started being measured on the basis of the 'success' of their entrepreneur class, though no remnant of the old 'gentleman' class distinction remained any more. Any one acquiring the material symbols of prosperity and affluence got accepted into the fold of successful and rich men. The libertarian ideology stood for encouraging full-fledged expression the creative-human-spirit of man !

The new democratic ruler class replaced the ancient Royal class, and the new-rich replaced the class of old Feudal and Noble classes ! New class-divisions, but unchanged energy-system and norms around the base class-gulfs. The more the things changed, the more the basics remained unchanged !

'Success' had become the new universal mantra, which was exclusively confined to the field of industrial and economic growth. Every other sector of human-activity naturally got side-lined. Fields like education and knowledge-creation etc. have become depended on the whims of the industrial and the newly emerged political class, who had clandestinely aligned with the industrial class for the above narrated one and only known model of country progress.

Today, the ambition of man goes much beyond having enough to eat, enough to dress, enough roof over the head to dwell-in, and a mate-for- life to live with. There are multiple layers of material success and style synthetically created in modern the living-system, that each person builds-up his particular desires and targets of growth and success in advance. It do not have anything to do with eat-more, dress-more, dwell in a house with more security, or marring super-woman for life etc. It is all about touching different, socially made myths of conceptual levels of SUCCESS ! Such levels of life and existence run parallel to the raw-needs and reality of life, in its existential relevance and meaning.

Every person who has attained some 'success' always looked-up to the next level, or class, as his next destination to reach. Every such class-distinction was marked by their special standard of luxury, by the kind of residential colonies they stay, the class of school they send their children, the company in which they and their families mix-up among many other such marks of their economic and social class. To enter the one-up class, what was essential was to internalize their values; the new language, the new facial expressions and body language, and possessing the new tangible objects around life.

Even the very bottom classes in every society also kept the above obsession, ie. of moving to the next economic and social ladder of success ! But, the speed-in which the top most classes proceeded to the next and next realms was unmatched for the bottom classes, chiefly because of the simple un-affordability of the kind of luxury items and symbols the former class was able to possess ! The very excessive supply of money in the market helped the top classes to reach such unattainable(for those who follow them) economic and class levels, that according to every authentic recent economic survey, more than 55% of world's wealth got landed in the hands of less than 1% elites of world population !

As the profit margins are exceedingly high while dealing in products and services for these rich class, few industries take interest in catering to the needs of the lower class. The exceedingly high-prices in the Housing market is the best example. Options for low-economic classed are almost Nil in the Housing market. Every best product and services go searching for the affluent profit-margin of the rich class, thus, pushing the inflation naturally, making even routine life needs of the bottom classes un-affordable to them !. (Please see blog on inflation caused due to this reason, at link: http://understandinginflationinanewlight.blogspot.in/2013/07/thecauses-inflation-simplified-or.html)

Mankind's arriving, or landing-up at such a state of, or standards of weird notions of SUCCESS has played havoc with the naturalness of human-life. It has distorted the original planes of human-activity, sense of equality and thought patterns. It has created grave issues around social-equality, as levels and criteria of equality has drastically altered. To reach such synthetic levels of success in society, men and women strive to become intentionally UNEQUAL, as at basic levels of eating, dressing, dwelling and mating, there are very limited or zero levels of showing-up one's up-man-ship, or living standards.

This is not to stand-against the paradigm of human-success and progress, but just to expose its evil and silly sides. Creativity is not limited into one or other chosen fields of human-activity. Institutionalizing human-creativity and its exalted-status in one or

two chosen fields would kill the unique and universal natural gift of every person, and its overall utility towards human-progress! In other words, encouraging and propagating HUMAN-EQUALITY will not kill the creative-human spirit in any manner. It would only bring-out the sacred-gift in every human-being in the long-run ! (Please share our blogs that depicts what kind of EQUALITY we mean for universally sustainable peace and happiness, at

link: http://whatequalityshouldmeanindemocracy.blogspot.in/)

In animal kingdom also we observe the inherent drive for exalting and DISPLAYING one's physical prowess...male-birds spreading their feathers and dancing to impress the other sex is common. Man had overcome many of our animal traits in the course of civilization, like the perennial fear of the other, and the resultant jungle like hostility to strangers. By realizing the folly that is in discuss here, we might be able to free ourselves from this also one day ! **One's excessively exhibited superiority and social-heights will stun and incapacitate those who are below-par, and unnecessarily create social tension. It alienates and separate those who below-par, into unhealthy social divides.**

Modern industry's very existence is depended upon manufacturing and catering to such different SUCCESS standards of modern citizens. Huge percentage of the total capital spending of each nation goes into meeting such higher living-standards of these elite-class, leaving bare minimum reserve for meeting the bare-life-needs of common-citizens. The latter class still live at the basic need level of existence !

No wonder, in case world is struck by large-scale natural, or man-made catastrophe, many of its elites will find it extremely difficult to come-down to the basic-need level life, due to their dependency on artificially learned and habituated needs. Modern world has turned human-life into an altogether different ball-game !

Article-4

Firm Classification of all violence in the world into TWO basic types !

Narration : Modern world is engaged in a rather futile attempt to understand the phenomenon of current terror and violence, especially in the Islamic world. This philosophic attempt, to get all the violence in human-history reduced into TWO basic type, might help to understand the cause of the calamity. One thing that conspicuously gets revealed is the vicious and nasty outcome of POWER of all sorts; it stuns minds, and turn normal human-beings into brutes.

(OR) How exceptionally one could be free, when he lets the other also free the same way he wants it to be for himself !

Modern world is full of violence, oppression, revolts and uprisings, despite the general claim that it is open, objective, free, individual-centered and transparent world ! Though the mainstream world picture these revolts and uprisings mostly as localized terrorist and anti-establishment acts, an attempt to **classify all violence and atrocities in the world**- whether past or present- would reveal that, atrocities and violence could be only of TWO basic types, transcending regions and nationalities:

(1) that unleashed by the **powerful** upon those who are under them,

(2) that of the **oppressed** against their oppressors. (oppressors are the powerful, or those who talk about the establishment in power or the mainstream world as if they represent it !)

Both the above groups, or rather 'mind-sets', (mind-set because, they are **not** permanent socio-economic groups, but who adopt the same values and attitude towards the other, when one is at either side of the wall at any time in life!) keep very valid reasons for unleashing violence on the other. **One things gets revealed as the central CAUSE of violence; it is the vicious and nasty human vice of acquiring POWER, and often institutionalize it in society !**

The rage of the powerful against those who are powerless

1) The despise and contempt of the powerful towards those who do not enjoy any share in power and resources needs no explanation ! One of the best examples is the atrocities unleashed by the higher caste-men over the lower-caste men in the not so ancient India. Few lower-castes were compulsorily designated to take-up certain kinds of ugly and lowly jobs, like carrying the 'night-soil' (faeces/faces) of the higher caste to distant location for disposal. Lower castes were not allowed to draw water from the common well of the village, and they could be harshly punished with extreme violence and death for breach of the custom.

In the southern states of India, the low-castes were supposed to loudly chant that 'ugly one' is approaching while on the common path, to warn the higher caste-men approaching from the opposite direction to keep -away from getting polluted by the formers physical proximity ! Their women were not allowed to cover breasts, because it was considered as a sign of assertion of dignified self-hood and freedom ! Lower caste women were not supposed to deny sex to the Brahmin(top caste) men whenever they demand it. Violence and death were very common for breaches of such traditions.

2) Another well evidenced example is the despise and contempt the Colonial nations meted out to the natives. The natives were as powerless as prisoners of war; an absolute property of those who held power and control over them. Every sign of assertion of freedom was brutally suppressed, and the perpetrators hanged, as allowing dissent was like allowing the seeds of freedom to sprout. **Freedom-demanding slaves were the most dangerous threat to the unhindered sense of self of the masters !**

Every sign of disobedience, or demand of anything resembling freedom and rights was brutally crushed at its very budding. What was most unbearable for the power-wielder was any sign of self-assertion from the part of the victims. So, the rage of the powerful against the power-less was a natural reality since the inception of man's history.

3) In the modern age, the best example of this disdain and contempt against the powerless could be cited to the dens of our Police and military forces. Whether it is in USA or in India, when a Police-man with the fierce power of the entire-state behind him engage with the 'people', the despise and contempt against them comes naturally. It is common knowledge these days that, most of the criminals in the world have acquired their criminal-mind-set from the jails. It is also now known that the seeds of the Islamic State (the ISIS) were born in the Iraqi jails, where native Iraqi men were kept, post US invasion (more about this relation is taken-up in a below para)

While one man to another man interaction is based on the compulsions of mutual acceptance at equal footing, interactions between a representative of the state, or with any similar impersonal center-of authority with an individual citizen, makes it fiercely impersonal and unequal, **like that between a man and a non-man.**

Every institutionalized power-center makes its interactions with single-citizens highly vulnerable to abuse and violations, and such victims of violation and abuse, in turn transform into violators and abusers themselves. This is the basic of every form of rights-violations and atrocity in the world.

4) The self-hatred of those who are perpetually under compulsion to obey orders, and to please the ones in power: This is a most central aspect of VIOLENCE from the camp of the oppressor. **A man, or a group of men under a powerful leader,or an institution/organization fueled by authority or**

power, loses, or simply abandon his/their rational and independent faculties and even the very SELF-HOOD in sheer desperation, because he/they are never let to use it as their-own! He is supposed to wait for orders from-up for his course of action. This is quite a damaging and dangerous mind-set that most men under absolute power suffer from.

The power source could be anything; say political power, power of the religious heads, power of the gang-leaders in underworld activities, or that of sheer-power of money in the corporate sector. They are often compelled to boot-lick, or show false-alliance and LOYALTY to the leader, fearing for his own life, or at least wishing for his-own special mercy, protection, and benefits from the leader/power-center. SYCOPHANCY is a modern-day ugly disease caused exclusively by the vice of power !

A vicious sense of self-hatred is the sure and certain psychological outcome from this situation, and these men will vent this frustration upon those who turn-up under them as 'victims' ! Violence and torture are mostly undertaken by these neurotic men, whether it is in war fields, terrorist camps or in Police stations. It is the extreme self-hatred of the abuser that gets a natural out-let when he/they torture their victims. Any one with some sense of self-esteem will find it very difficult to violate other-human beings !

<u>The rage of the vanquished against the oppressors</u>

History of man will stand confused and perplexed to decide whose rage was more cruel; that of the traditional powerful over the powerless, or that of the vanquished and oppressed against their oppressors!
Violence is just violence. It has only one language, but two distinct mind-sets, as we have seen above.

But one thing is conspicuous about this 2nd type of violence; i**t always arise as a natural reaction to the first-type, ie. as a reaction of the oppressed against the acts of the oppressor !**

The best example of the extreme rage of the oppressed over their oppressors in recent history was that of French revolution. Common citizens sat as prosecutors and judges, with Guillotines kept-ready nearby, to execute even their oppressor King and Queen ! Heads rolled every hour of the day, while ordinary men and women of France kept counting them !

In the Indian freedom struggle also, there were many ambushes against the British soldiers enacted by the oppressed Indian citizens. Take the history, and we will find equal number of such uprising by the oppressed men against their oppressors to the oppressive acts of the power-holders.

One thing to be specially noted about the state of mind of the oppressed is that, it takes-away all his sense of humanness from him. Human-mind, though it could be kept under subjugation for long-periods through continued acts of oppression and atrocities, given a chance, it would bounce-back with equal ferocity as that of the oppressor ! Probably, it is because of the learning of this vital lesson that mankind could enact land-mark Declarations and Bills of the Rights of man after the American and French Revolutions. These bills declared and enacted that, Freedom and Liberty are inalienable, natural rights of man that no-one can take it away from him. All further political systems and organizations that man had set-up in the world were specifically meant for, and aimed at restricting the very such governmental forms from meddling with this vital Freedom of man.

But, the central question is, have the world and her vital political and social establishments, systems and institutions really adhering to the above land-mark paradigm shift in the attitude and ideology about respecting and keeping in-tact the above vital finding ?

Answer is, a sad no ! Even today, even in our most acclaimed democratic nations in the world, the freedom, personal liberty and dignity of citizens are kept only in the book ! Basically, the concept of the old POWER-STATE is what runs the show, and hence Power and Rights (freedom/liberty/individual dignity) are two opposite poles, the status of ordinary citizen is same as its was under any other older, third-party (rule by Kings and his likes) regimes of the past.

Whether it is in the street, jails or in various government vs. citizen interaction points, common citizens are treated like old 'subjects' !

So, whatever violence and atrocities that we have today from various parts of the world could be directly attributed to the 2nd kind that we have seen in the beginning, that is the acts of violence of the oppressed against the oppressor !

Oppression, and lack of acceptance of the dignified-self of man simply will result in plain violence if not today, at some point in future. The oppressed always gets out of his sense of reason and balance, and social order will be brought-back only after annihilation of the oppressor, or at least the oppressor too made to suffer all the humiliation, disparity and contempt that they once suffered.

A repeat look at each act of major violence in modern world

Take for example, the current ISIS, Boko-Haram, or the Yemeni uprising, to see into what category above, we could classify them ? Are they the oppression of the mighty and powerful over those who are under them, or are they the counter-fight of the oppressed and the vanquished, against their oppressors ? A frank clinical analysis of the emotions involved in these fights and violence would enable mankind to find a clear answer.

Let us first closely look at the profile of men who typically join ISIS. Stories from post American occupation Iraqi jails say that, the seeds of ISIS, including the emergence of the so called, self-proclaimed Caliphate of the envisioned Global Islamic state-Al-Baghdadi-had sprouted from there !(We mentioned it once in one of the above paragraphs)

In a recent (December last week, 2014) article by Martin Chulov appeared in the Indian magazine 'The week', one Abu Ahmed, an IS Jihadist he had interviewed said:

' IS wouldn't have emerged if US hadn't attacked Iraq, and detained and kept large number of suspects in prisons' .

Al Baghdadi, the current alleged IS leader, was a co-prisoner with the said Abu Ahmed in one of the Iraqi detaining center. The prison life enabled these men to connect with each other regularly ,and give rise to IS !

Another recent story (in Indian Express newspaper, 15th April, 2015) about Maldives, from where about 200 Jihadists had joined ISIS, reports that most of them were from the lower-strata of society, who used to indulge in 'sin'.(drugs, alcohol and street-crimes) Those who are forced to live at the peripherals of modern society anywhere in modern world, suffer from that serious symptom of 'non-belonging'; comfortable life all over the world means life with air-conditioned rooms, well-paid jobs in multinational companies, servants at home, financial capacity to send children to reputed schools, and owning of top-model cars and other house-hold articles etc. Those who cannot afford these standard comforts of modern life starts isolating themselves from the mainstream. They miserably fail to identify themselves with the so called real-world out-side, but experience the natural, existential pressure of identifying themselves with the essential oneness with life that no one can escape from.

This irrefutable inner-pressure of each human-being to get-integrated with life in some way or other, after failing to do it with anything that exists around them, compels them to seek, first-of all, an identity with whatever they had born into, and grown-up with. Let it be the peculiar cultural-upbringing, language, religious-myths and rituals, food-habits and social-traditions...it is a going back to the roots. No open mind can refuse to see the absolute similarity of those who join ISIS and similar other Jihadi organizations and outfits with the above said phenomenon.

Every human-being wishes to progress, improve-upon what they have been practicing in the past. But, as said above, when they fail to do so, due to the total alien features of whatever is available around, they have nowhere else to go-back except to their roots ! This is exactly what is behind the ISIS and similar 'Islamist' movement world witness today. See the close similarity of this, with what Hindus do in India; they intent to unite together in an unprecedented way, and attain supremacy of their way of life and believes upon every other in the country, if possible, over the entire world !

Once these men go back to their roots, it is mandatory that they get indulged into all its diabolic, primeval acts and practices. If brutal assassination of human-beings was not alien to old Islamic, tribal culture, ensuring purity of blood and culture of the population by eliminating 'outsiders' was also not alien to old Hindu culture. So, assigning the cause of ISIS and other Islamist violence to the teachings and doctrines of Islam might be, to the best logical analysis, erroneous. The root fact could be the failure of the majority world population to find 'belongingness' with the values, norms, ways, available roles, and practices of the contemporary world. It is a world where only a small minority feel belongingness.

One thing is doubtless: the violence and atrocities that the ISIS and other similar outfits exhibit in the modern world do not belong to the first-type of violence that we have seen in the beginning, ie. of the oppressors. These men, perhaps subjectively, perceive a kind of isolation from the mainstream world, that today, predominantly is a Western world, with all its typical symbols of development and advancement !It is well evident from the very recent, reliable statistics and research studies that, such Western-ways of world-development and advancement naturally create exclusive pockets of affluence, resulting in ever increasing accumulation of wealth and resources into fewer and fewer hands. As per latest research results,(Oxfam and Zurich University studies) almost 55% of the world's wealth is concentrated in the hands of less than 1% affluent families !Please share the emotional catastrophe of such a world of economic and socio-political order at blog-

post: http://closedmodernworlddespitedemocracy.blogspot.in/ .

With their exclusive claims on science and its fruits, a general abandonment of religion and spiritual-realities of life- but treating life purely in its empirical aspects etc., the western way has become the mainstream way of life in the modern world. It is now well-known that through Colonialism, what Europe had overtly intended was 'civilizing' the rest of the world, though in reality, it was naked conquest.

 Those communities and regions in the world where the above ways of the west have not yet crept-in, tend to consider it a direct, external assault, or threat to their localized beliefs, customs and traditions. For them, it is a kind of cultural assault, and even violence !

The below paragraph, that talks about the 'subjective' aspects of both the oppression, and also being under-oppression, might throw some additional light to find right answers to the question raised above:

The subjective aspects about both of the 'oppressor', and that of being under-oppression

 The above assertion was made with the clear awareness and understanding that, many a times, the sense of both the oppression,(from the part of the oppressors) as well as that of insubordination or dissent from the part of those who hold some or other kind of **power,**(the oppressor**)** most often, is purely subjective. Means, the cause behind the violence unleashed by the oppressed against the deemed 'oppressor', (the power-holder) and that behind the terror and oppression unleashed against the dissenters and trouble-makers by the power-holder or the establishment, might be purely subjective. It is the 'sense' of oppression, and also the sense of insubordination and dissent is what trigger violence and terror acts ! The fear factor, that of the ones in Power about those who are supposed to be 'under' it, concerning their adherence and subordination, and that of the oppressed about the oppressor concerning the fate of his prized liberty is the chief cause behind all the violence in the world ! Hope no one could raise any sensible objection against the above arrived crucial conclusion.

As we have arrived at a very specific classification of all the violence that takes place between two men or two groups of men in the world, now let us attempt to arrive at a similar inference, as to what causes a person or a group to put another man or group under some or other kind of authority or power, and restrict his/their freedom as it was once enjoyed by all at equal footing ? We must understand it first, because, out of the TWO types of violence seen above, **it is the FIRST type that always takes place first.** The second type always takes place as a reaction to the first !

Why and how early men started treating the 'other' as a threat and botheration ?

When we take-up this important question for analysis, that is, why individual man and human-societies always show tendency to keep other men and other communities under control and submission, the first answer we receive is that, **it is the law of nature**! There are ample evidences from our old existing jungles that might support the said view; at jungles, the physically, or the number-wise strong always hold the upper-hand in animal societies, whether in the matter of geographical space, food and water resources, or sexual mate.

In human-society also, history has full of stories about powerful warriors, tribes and kingdoms of the past conquering and defeating lesser powerful men, groups and kingdoms.

But at a final analysis, equally valid historical data compel us to discard the above 'natural-law' inference on following grounds:

1) For reasons yet unknown, it was mostly the larger and stronger animals and their species that had already vanished, or in the process of fast extinct from the face of earth. Take the example of the already extinct species of dinosaurs and similar large bodied species and birds, gradually vanishing large and strong bodied species like Lions and Tigers etc. If the hegemony of the strong was the law of nature, she wouldn't have allowed such a breach of law.

Even if we accept that, the criteria of 'survival' was not exactly that of superior physical- strength of the species but that of their capability for 'adaptation' to the always changing physical environment, let us try to see the plain falsehood of this argument: The same author argues at his blog: http://leadingdogmasthatruletheworld.blogspot.in/2012/08/introduction-world-may-appear-as.html :

" the individual member, (of any species) whether an animal, or a plant, is a helpless 'object' of various energies and strategies of nature. The 'member' cannot ever wish, or 'will' to 'mutate', (to adapt to a changed environment) so that a more developed offspring could come out of him/her. Hence, the entire responsibility to produce a better adapted offspring rests exclusively with the same NATURE !

The species are absolutely BLIND about the possibility of evolution. **The hero, or the villain here is, the same 'nature' ! This is serious philosophical dilemma that the evolutionists must address. After all, who is the beneficiary of evolution ? If we believe modern science, the natural immunity of man, animals and plants against diseases is constantly on the down fall ! How would this empirical evidence substantiate evolution if its chief goal was more evolved, and more adapted species ? The question ' into what ultimate state evolution leads to ?' becomes very relevant here"**

What adapts to the changed environment is NOT any individual member of the species (by its 'conscious' will) but Nature herself, as a temporary strategy to the then changed environment ! The actor or the ant-hero in the game is 'nature' herself !

As the subject of this post is not 'evolution' as its is, let us leave it here, and proceed with our chief objective; answering the question of why man and groups show tendency to over-power other men and groups.

2) If we look at human history too, all the strong-men, tribes and nations of the past have perished absolutely !No reasonable remnant of the old Rome, Ottoman, Napoleon's or German (Hitler's) empire exists today. World, if seen at closer and clinical angles, is gradually moving towards a more and more egalitarian and inclusive kind of society in its broad sense and meaning, though it is far-away from a turning a perfect one in any sense.

So, the hegemony of the 'strong' and powerful is the 'natural-law' argument fails on every count.

Why then man and communities tend to hold-power and control over other men and other groups ?

If we very closely analyse the first kind of violence, that we have concluded as that always takes place first, we will find that what tends the oppressor to oppress others is his fear of losing his LIBERTY to do what he likes, if he lets the other person or persons to do what he likes ! Own liberty and freedom is always depended upon the degree of liberty and freedom of others around. My physical space, my mate and my food would, most of the time, be considered as his space, his mate and his food by the other person too. This naturally will lead to unpleasant and even bloody fights. So, if I want to have my unbound freedom and liberty, it is absolutely necessary that I find a way to curtail the liberty and freedom of the other person !

Rousseau had beautifully explained the above existential dilemma of the primeval man, and the solution he found, in his book,' On the origin of inequality': (p.78, The great books foundation, Chicago, 1955)

" the rich man, thus urged by necessity, conceived at length the profoundest plan that ever entered the mind of man: this was to employ in his favour the forces of those who attacked him, to make allies of his adversaries, to inspire them with different maxims, and to give them other institutions as favourable to himself, as the law of nature was unfavourable.....

"Let us join", said he, " to guard the weak from oppression,to restrain the ambitious, and secure to every man the possession of what belongs to him: let us institute rules of justice and peace, to which all without exception may be obliged to conform........

In short, 'such was, or may well have been, the origin of society and law, which bound new fetters on the poor, and gave new powers to the rich, which irretrievably destroyed natural liberty, eternally fixed the law of property and inequality, converted clever usurpation into unalterable right, and for the advantage of a few ambitious individuals, subjected all mankind to perpetual labour, slavery and wretchedness"

Rousseau had attributed it to the sinful beginning of modern civil society and government. A similar story of this author could be found at blog-post: http://originofestablishment.blogspot.in/

In the absence of any better explanation and theory, we have to share the above conclusion that, man started restraining the liberty of other men, and human-society in general, exclusively for the need of ensuring own freedom the most secure and sustainable way ! The liberty of other man in the same degree as that of mine would always be a hindrance to my own liberty and freedom ! As seen and explained in very detail in this author's blog-post referred above, institutions of permanent social divisions (two permanent class of men,- or two mind-sets- divided between a great wall) had occurred around the above fundamental selfish motive and emotions of primeval man.
Our blog; http://direneedofreinventingdemocracy.blogspot.in/2014/06/it-is-high-time-to-rethink-on.html, explains this phenomenon in more detail.

Instead of excluding the other person and group from having his rights and liberty too in the life-scheme on earth, what got institutionalized in human-society was a **great wall of separation** between a group that always talked in first-person about the society and establishment, while about those who are on the other-side of the wall, as 'subjects' under the establishment, or the organized society, with a fundamental obligation and duty to live under the supremacy of the former group. Permanent values and traditions got cemented in human-society of future, about the roles and obligations of whoso ever happened at each side of the wall. **Like the cementing of patriarchal traditions in the man-women relation in human-society, the establishment and subject relation also got cemented in human-society permanently ! Though there occurred many loosening-up in the man-woman relation as human-civilization advanced, very little has been changed in the man and establishment tie.**

The yet unknown and unrealized kind of freedom and liberty in human-relations when both parties let each other go absolutely uninhibited and free !

The crux of what we have gathered from the above discussion and the reference materials presented
(Rousseau's stand, and this authors blog-post) was that, the first acts of oppression, or the act of isolating the questioning or the freedom seeking 'other' from the group was caused by the reluctance of the primeval man to be 'inclusive' in his behaviour and attitude towards the 'other'. With his animal like primordial mind, nothing other than caring the need and interests of the self was possible for him ! **He could only fear, and be apprehensive of the 'other', that if he allows him to be one with the group, he might turn an enemy of his self-interest, and his absolute freedom in future.** So, he took maximum precaution, to see the 'other' ousted from the group, or to be trapped under the pretext of social and political laws or norms, so that he always remain a lesser threat to his-own freedom. Simply put, the starting point of despise, contempt and even initiating violence against the 'other' was the result of primordial, animal like fear of human-beings.

When someone treats you with fear and apprehension in his mind, you can not react as if you do not fear, and have apprehension about the other too. But if one could get-rid of such primitive fears and apprehensions about the other, with own consciously-put intellectual and rational effort, the 'other' too react the same way, the interaction and relation gets into an altogether open, free and unprecedented mode ! Self-expression peaks from both the parties, and the open and receptive mood of both, opens-up an uninhibited and free stream of exchange!
When fear escapes from the mind about the other, a kind of exceptional confidence grips both the parties, and it might be difficult to believe for those who had never experienced such free and open-exchange of minds, each one expresses in such a way that they themselves wonder from whom and where such unprecedented colours and features of own self come from ? This is especially true with intimate relation between opposite sexes; when there is no bound for self-expression, such relations reaches unprecedented and mysterious realms of self-expression ! Such mysterious sense of freedom and liberty must have been the cause behind great work of art, literature and poetry in human-history.

'Self' is always a kind of tightness of one's nerves, a kind of resistance or armor, kept to ward of the other, or to protect oneself from others ! When one gets free, or gets liberated from the need for such armor and resistance, a free-flow of natural energies occur, and involved parties get an opportunity to experience the real power and possibilities of uninhibited human-interaction and relation.

Prejudices, dogmas, and practices that needed to be discarded from society to achieve such free-flowing human-exchange

1) Pretension of one's superiority under some or other garbs: Exhibition of one's some or other superiority is nothing but a direct form of violence against those who does not share it; let it be the way one is dressed, his high-social status, his economic high-status, or his share in the political or other power-basket.

Such all-around inequality in the general way of life, share-in the power factor, institutionalized superiority of any-one religion, language or caste, culture etc, without fail, act as disguised form of violence and abuse.

2) superstition or dogma that what one has in the form of personal bodily features, riches and special abilities are his-own make, or achievement attained by his self-effort, or that of his ethnic group/nation

The existing myths, norms and traditions about SUCCESS in life also equally make some men superior than those who could not achieve success in the same degree. Such permanent features in society also acts as a form of violence and abuse over those who are far below in the ladder of SUCCESS.

3) Inability to consider and accept whatever is unique about the other person/other community/group, and resistance to share whatever is common in the world as common-right of all persons in the world, or others in the same community.

Present world consider only certain forms of ability or propensity meritorious, say, the entrepreneurship skills. Unlike in the early days of direct barter, the tiller needed to accept and respect the work and profession of the baker as well as that of the butcher, otherwise life would have become stand-still. But today, the tiller himself can act as baker, butcher and a in a hundred other roles, in his highly acclaimed entrepreneur-ship skill. Those who do not possess that skill in considerable degree are looked-down upon in modern society, in spite of his mastery in many other fields without which the entrepreneur-class can not perform well. Such institutionalized inequality about professions also acts as indirect form of violations in modern world.

4) Contempt towards the 'other' who do not own things in equal quantity with that of mine: This is the confidence and pride of the successful that they are more

blessed, more chosen or 'selected' by nature as per Darwin's survival of the fittest' theory ! The other who are deprived and suffer the pains of life, undergo it because they didn't work-hard, and not acted as smartly as the former. So, it is better to leave them at nature's own mercy, while minding own-business in a practical and smart-strategy of detachment ! I mind my business, while letting the other to mind his business, forgetful of what life-situation the other person or other community live-in.

Final answer is that, if any person or community/ institution violate the sense of dignity and self-hood of any other person or group, in any manner, it will definitely result in turning such other person /community a violator and an aggressor some time in future !

Some clue into the ultimate principle, or law of nature about man vs man relation

It was clearly and undoubtedly NOT the plain survival of the fittest in the world, in its physical and Darwinist sense, while judging from the evidences in history that we have once seen above. The strong and mighty always perished earlier than the weak and the meek in history, in its long-term effect. So, such a belief or theory, we will be forced to conclude that, might have been the outcome of a particular remnant of our primeval, animal propensities ! The very goal, task and process of human-civilization was to free man from such jungle values, notions and practices, and mankind had succeeded a lot in the said task. But, the task is still incomplete to a large degree...we may have to identify and realize our subconscious(primeval) urge to keep the other-man subjugated to our will, in order to free-ourselves from this jungle urge !

We could well recognize that, when one is absolutely free, (free from subjugation to another's will) what he feel about the other, how stranger he might be, would be only a healthy curiosity to know more about him, not any jungle type fear and animosity. Therefore, to help the emergence of a new, more healthy world-order, we must find a way out to end her existing fear of the other, and man's subconscious wish to subjugate him to his will, by some or other pretext. The avenues of developing a new and more healthy, modern attitude towards the 'other' is very much there in human-capacity, and his intelligence sphere.

Recommend the following links to know more about what has been proposed above: http://newphilosophyoflife.blogspot.in/
http://closedmodernworlddespitedemocracy.blogspot.in/
http://leadingdogmasthatruletheworld.blogspot.in/

Article-5

Modern Democracy : The net essence of its evils

There was an article in the 'Indian Express' news paper on November 17th, 2014, wherein the author had a sentence that explained the essence of the evil that modern democracies are infected with; He was referring to the issue of abandoning 'death penalty' altogether from the judicial system of nations.

" The Indian parliament is not sensitive to such matters" !

Not only Indian parliament, but every modern political state treats single individual merely as an **impersonal component** in the greater whole, the society, or the country.. Let him live or die, the State is not sensitive, or centrally concerned about such issues. This is a grave philosophical, or to be more right, an ontological malady of modern political and social theory.

Do modern states represent whatever is noble and pious about the humankind ? Do they solely and directly exist to achieve the grooming of better communities, and an ideal larger world ?

Even though in paper it appears so, in reality, thanks to their predominant POLITICAL nature, they are entirely distinct entities, with their professional goal and work-dynamics remaining far remote from everything pious and noble ! What these modern political entities keep and practice is a kind of 'state-craft', an old art and science of managing mass human communities within the frame-work of the old 'ruler and the ruled' paradigm. The myths and norms around the older authoritarian third-party regimes (in the sense that rulers were altogether different a class, or species from that of the people !) around the 'ruler and the ruled' are still active and alive at this realm.

Noam Chomsky was candid about the present regimes' prejudices about people's class:

" If you read the sayings of the founding fathers,(of America) you will discover that, that was essentially their view as well. **They also regarded**

the public as a dangerous threat. **The way the country ought to be organized, as John Jay put it, the president of the constitutional** convention and the first supreme court- chief justice of the supreme court, his- one of his favorite maxims, according to his biographer, was that those who run- those who own the country ought to govern it. And if they can't govern it by force, they've got to govern it in another way, and that ultimately requires deception, propaganda, indoctrination, the manufacture of consent" (Chomsky, in a speech delivered at University of Wisconsin - Madison, March 15, 1989)

He says, while the communist regimes have the 'club' (totalitarian power)in their hands to discipline the 'internal enemies'- the people, what suits democracy is the above said 'deception by propaganda, indoctrination and manufactured consent'. In principle, both methods are equal for the intended purpose.

Modern democratic regimes are modeled exactly the same way that any old third-party
(authoritarian) regimes were modeled, with regard to their attitude towards people !

Democracy as a peoples own political system had never attempted, nor thought-out, or produced any different set of norms, values and myths that amply suited a real regime of people . The only paradigm shift that was achieved by the government of people was about the ones who should occupy the seats of power; instead of Kings, Feudal-Lords, or any hierarchical ruling class, democracy insisted on seating peoples representatives there on these seats !

It was a great tragedy for human-kind as this un-thought tenet has taken away the opportunity for a grass-root change, as to what should be the real status and role of citizens class under the peoples own system !!! So, peoples' class still remain as the old class of 'subjects' under modern democratic regimes, as passive victims, targets or even predators' prey under all the follies and tyranny of the modern 'ruling' class ! A new class of RULERS in the form of professional political leaders and their well organized groups are there well set and established, in every modern nation where democracy reigns.

The question of hanging or not hanging criminals is one in a thousand of similar crucial questions that modern democratic states fail to take-up in the new light of a true regime of people !

What Albert Camu (a Nobel prized author) had said deserves central attention here:

"an age can be called modern and progressive only when it starts sending her prisoners to mental asylums than jails". Forget about the past third-party regimes; a peoples own governmental system should have taken-up with serious concern, as to what makes ordinary individual a criminal, or anti-social. It should not have been considered a merely a law and order issue, but a psychological, or a social science issue. Only when such grass-root level understanding takes place in modern democratic system, that we could claim our governmental system as truly and genuinely 'democratic', or something under a peoples own government-model.

Friedrich Hayek describes what could be such freedom under peoples own government: (*The Collected Works of F. A. Hayek*, Vol. 10: *Socialism and War: Essays, Documents, Reviews* (Chicago: University of Chicago Press, 1997), Chapter 11: "The Intellectuals and Socialism," [1949], pp. 221-237)

" If the cause of liberty is to prevail once again, it is necessary for friends of freedom to not be afraid of being radical in their case for classical liberalism – even "Utopian" in a right meaning of the term.[27] To once more make it a shining and attractive ideal to imagine **a world of free men who are no longer slaves to others, whether they be monarchs or majorities…**

.. It would be a world of sovereign individuals who respect each other, who treat each other with dignity and who view each other as an end in himself, **rather than one of those pawns to be moved and sacrificed on that chessboard of society to serve the ends of another who presumes to impose coercive control over his fellow human beings"**

We have been into research and advocacy on the above theme for over 5 years, and have produced many papers dedicated to the cause of 'reinventing modern democracy'.. We are glad to share few of them with you here, at links: http://direneedofreinventingdemocracy.blogspot.in/ http://thecalamityofmoderndemocraticpolitics.blogspot.in/ http://democracywithoutpoliticalparties.blogspot.in/ http://anewtheoryondemocraticestablishment.blogspot.in/

Article-6

It is high-time to rethink on the compatibility of 'Power-State' model for democracy

Introduction

America invaded Iraq to restore democracy in that country, after killing its despotic ruler, Saddam Hussein. There were leading news-item in every world newspaper recently (12th June, 2014) that the Sunni rebels of the present government in Iraq captured major cities in the state, and thousands of families are fleeing to safer pockets of the country.

The rebels in Syria have been fighting a similar battle with the present ruler for many years now, to oust him and establish a different government.

Egypt has got her third President elected recently, after the bloody ouster of two in the span of 3 years !

Isn't it most sensible to reduce these constant phenomenon of bloody fights for grabbing political power, or to occupy the ruler's seat in the democratic world into its singular fundamental cause ? Though the cause that we propose here might look a bit philosophical, common sense of even ordinary persons would agree to it that, it deserves serious rethinking on the compatibility of 'power-state' model for democracy, the celebrated governmental system of EQUAL MEN.

Power has the following universal traits:

1) It enables its holders to have absolute freedom
2) Power-holders' freedom is gained chiefly by the lesser freedom of those who are under the spell of it.

One's restricted freedom is caused chiefly due to his need to accept similar freedom of others. I can not have my absolute frcc-ways whcn others also do enjoy similar freedom. Therefore, under the spell of institutionalized or other forms of power, others enjoy lesser or no freedom at all, and then my freedom gains an absolutely free domain !I am the law maker, hence no one under ordinary circumstances will dare to question me. Therefore, I am free to care or not care for the freedom of others. In paper democracy, freedom is same for both the law makers and the ordinary citizen. But the fear of the power of the fiercely impersonal State often subjugate citizens, and force them to be silent.

3) It naturally grooms subjugation, and even develop worshiping tendencies in those who are under it, because, for the victims of power, subjugation, sycophancy and even worship only would ensure protection and favors. In many Indian States, followers of leaders often prostate before them, and touch their feet to express absolute subjugation and surrender !

4) Every human child grows-up listening to glorified stories about Kings, Queens and similar members of the Ruler class. Hence, every human-being unconsciously keep a secret desire to occupy seats of Power someday, so that they could enjoy the kind of freedom those Kings and Queens used to have. Modern democratic order gives ample opportunity even for ordinary citizens to dream big, and fulfill these dreams if they work hard. But such fulfillment of pathological desires should not have had any place in a governmental system of equal men (democracy) !

5) Power usually claims of its ability to achieve instant changes in society, simply on its above listed strengths. But by all logic, such advantages of Power suffers heavily on the ground of its multitude of draw-backs with regard to the general peril of freedom and rights of the ordinary citizens. It is enemy number one of true democracy, if it is to remain a genuine governmental system of Equal Men.

Power is not the one and only fuel for bringing forth revolutionary social and political changes in the world. The best example is just in-front of us, in our own country; the successful struggle for independence led by Mahatma Gandhi against the great British Empire ! The idea of inalienable individual freedom and liberty that the American revolution had brought in also had its real roots in the writings of philosophers like John Locke and David Hume.

Bringing an end to the evil of Slavery was rather a personal mission of Abraham Lincoln. He had to fight a serious civil war with his own country men to bring-in the revolutionary law of banning slave trade. He later clarified his actual definition of a true democracy; ' As I won't be a slave, I won't be a master too, and this explains my idea of democracy'. His words express his clear stand against the present trend of choosing our 'masters' through elections in modern democracy.

6) It is advocated that in the absence of power, chaos and disorder will prevail. We have taken up this case in one of the portions below, to show that delinquency of every type emerges from power and power abuse. In other words, chaos and disorder appears in societies that have been under some or other kind of long spell of absolute power. Humankind

was never tested for no-power kind of social structure in history. But the isolated examples of customer behavior at modern malls and shopping centers etc., where they are free to pick up merchandise of their choice and then pay later at counters etc. should be treated as note-worthy model to forecast similar human behavior of citizens in a control free social atmosphere. When people are accepted and recognized as trust worthy, they tend to behave that way, with unprecedented responsibility. Most likely, they will show more responsibility and maturity to voluntarily obey all social norms and ethos.

7) Power kills, or blocks originality and creativity. Under Power-regimes, creativity and originality are supposed to be the exclusive privilege of those who are on the power-chairs. The ones under the spell of power take all pains to conceal their creativity and originality, to block the wrath of the masters ! What the power holders want is mere support and adulation of their ideas, and they always show the tendency to hate, and even destroy every sign of creativity from others. It threatens their sense of superiority ! (Following blog link throws light on how Power and authority kills originality and creativity in modern organizations; http://perilofreason.blogspot.in/

The stories of world famous despots, killing and eliminating the best minds (artists, scientists, innovators etc) the moment they occupy the Power-chair are popular. (Eg. Russian and similar revolution stories in history)

Under what logic, democracy- the governmental system of equal men- should keep a Power-state model ?

A government when formed through the democratic process of election, and when it holds the State power as it was usual during the old regimes, every one under such Power-regime, especially the political opponents, always has to bear with power abuses of varying degree, because, power has its psychological, institutional and traditional grip upon those who are under it. No institution or law is capable of standing against Power, whether it is in the hands of a monarch, a despot, or a democratic ruler ! Despite the prevalence of democracy for many centuries in the world, it could not produce any alternative governance model, fit exclusively for the governmental system of equal men.Hence, the ones who could not make it to the throne always nurture power-ambitions, (as power is the only real way to have complete FREEDOM for the seeking individual, and his group) and adopt various means to achieve their goal.

Armed attempt is one of such methods to take over Power. A ruler holding POWER is always an existential threat to every one under it. The threat may not be always real, but many times it is imaginary too . But the end outcome would be always the same; ie armed opposition to the throne, terrorist tactics, guerrilla war-fare, or ethnic conflicts with the throne for separate statehood etc. We have ample examples in the current history of modern world. Besides the examples of Iraq and Syria referred above, we had the bloody story of the annihilation of the Tamil separatists in Sri Lanka in the recent past by the ruling native government. In Nigeria, the Boko Haram radical Islamist group want to take over state power, and rule the nation under hard-line Islamic laws. In every case, what the rebels want is total hold on governmental power, so that they could have their own ways ! Through the medium of modern state power, one can have his own unlimited ways, whatever it might be. State power is the ultimate means for having ultimate freedom for oneself and his group. Every one who could pose threat to my freedom is now under my absolute control, so there is no hindrance at all for my, or my group's freedom. Now on, it is my will and my way all the way; absolutely !

Think of a total paradigm shift. If world could produce myths and values around a true governmental system of Equal men as per a totally altered democratic system and values ? What if future States are constituted without the mandatory element of POWER to govern nations of EQUAL MEN ?

It is plain common sense, cause-effect paradigm that delinquency is always caused as a pathological reaction against misplaced use of power. No animal is known to submit to power and authority of another unrelated animal without coercion. It was always involuntarily enforced upon the less powerful, and the latter oblige to submission out of utter necessity, or for the fear of cruelty, or even death from the hands of those who holds power !. So, delinquency could easily be understood as a mental condition caused directly by the existence of power as an inevitable malady in society. Power nullifies the entities of the ones under its spell. It can never accept the value and dignity of the other party. Power is a primordial evil force of the remote past. It should never have been adopted as the fuel in a governmental system of equal men-democracy. When it is present, no term of equality, rights or liberty could co-exist with it, in every practical and real term. Failure to recognize this chemical or physical law, is at the bottom our age's massive failure at peace and equality efforts.

A future enlightened world could be visualized only when such societies completely oust power-concepts from their governance principles and systems, by some of other means.

As there was no alternative value, or myth about governing masses and nations sans the fuel of Power, even when the once oppressed members in society managed to defeat their oppressors and then constitute their kind of establishment, they too adopt the same old Power-ways of their one time oppressors; ie. using, or enjoying the sinful sense of Power to the maximum ! The fate of the communist regimes is the best example. Their leaders who fought capitalistic masters and occupied the Power-chairs of States had no alternative model to govern people other than the same old Power-way. Hence, every communist government ended up adopting the capitalistic Power-way, or perished without achieving their cherished egalitarian goals !

Unfortunately, human societies today are at loss to think of anything beyond a governmental system of Power, let it be the exclusive governmental system of EQUAL HUMAN BEINGS, ie. democracy !

Think of how human civil society traditions managed to establish sustainable norms about garbage disposal, or electricity and water distribution. Or, how mankind had managed in educating their young with knowledge of the past generations ? It was able to eradicate many self-destructive evil traditions like polygamy, unequal status of women in etc. in societies. Similarly, once we could recognize and accept that, institutionalized state power does dreadful harm to every society than any good, we could eradicate it, and think of a hundred alternative ways and systems to self-govern our collective affairs, without the intervention of coercive POWER !.

Think of the excellent way in which modern societies manage their corporate governance. Sense of responsibility and self-excellence are adequate, natural inspirational tools for men to achieve excellent result with their given goals, as well as to create never heard creative means to achieve such goals !

Any single human-being when entrusted with institutionalized state power, involuntarily transform himself into a monster. He loses all his individualistic traits that makes him a single-unit in society. From now on, he represents the fiercely impersonal State. Despise and contempt towards the unattached single individuals, helpless and powerless, comes to him naturally !

Violence of every kind originates only in two exclusive ways; one as the natural revenge of the oppressed towards their oppressor, and two, that emerge in the power-holders from the despise and contempt towards the powerless individuals, especially those who dare to stand against, or question the authority of the power holder. Both parties see their victims not as single individuals, but as part of a greater evil whole.As it is obvious, power, especially institutionalized Power, is at the root cause of every kind of violence in the world, and the chief threat to world peace !.

The ones who had suffered under some or other kind of Power-atrocity, do develop one of the following reaction patterns towards life and the 'others' in society:

1) Learn to bear with after internalizing the power-atrocities, so that he never reacts, but exist peacefully with its evil ways. They even believe that Power is a necessary evil in every society, for its orderly functioning.

They kill their sense of self-hood, and attempt to live like a nullified entity. The slaves under the old colonial masters had adopted this method, it appears. From this groups, many a pathological, neurotic illness also take birth. These men practice to live entity-less lives out of necessity. Some of these men take to various kinds of crimes too, as without their already annihilated sense of self, they get immune to such sentiments of other men too. Hence, they get free from every sense of remorse and guilt. They face life like life-less machines.

2) The fire of the sense of self of man is never extinguishable. Even after thousand years of captivity and oppression, the flames of freedom and unhindered self-hood takes buds, and attempt to annihilate the oppressor. A moment of slackness from the part of the master-oppressor kindle such flame, and revenge is taken upon the oppressor.

3) Lie down and pretend subjugation. This group goes on planning their counter attack clandestinely, and adopt gorilla tactics and secret army tactics every day. Modern trait of terrorism could be classified into this category. This group know that an equal strength strike is never possible against the powerful oppressor, hence a prolonged but never ending armed agitation would bring best results. For this group, even an imaginary sense of powerlessness before the powerful is enough to plan their strategies and strikes. This involves an extreme hatred too, towards the ways and cultures of the powerful, or the oppressor. The hatred of the Muslim terror groups against the much powerful Western powers, seems to be a manifestation of this kind of a reaction against Power.

Power need not be always that of armed power. It could be the power of money and resources too

Powerlessness suffered by modern man is not always from the despising and neglectful attitude of modern democratic regimes towards ordinary citizens. The sentiments expressed by the US population recently, by the name' Occupy Wall street' etc., saying that it is the struggle of the oppressed 99% against the all controlling 1% elites in the capitalistic nation is one best example. The agitator's claim has much substance too, if the latest researches on inequality undertaken by many reputed institutions like Oxfam, Zurich University and others are to be believed. All such research studies reveal that more than 50% of world's wealth and resources are in the pockets of merely 70 or 90 rich business families or groups in the world !

This trend of more and more money and resources getting accumulated in the hands of fewer and fewer people every year was always known as a clear trend of modern capitalism. The majority of the world who are fated to compete for sharing the remaining 50% wealth and resources that fall from the table of the rich and powerful, a sure and certain feature of modern Capitalism, naturally create large scale aspiration for full-scale freedom and equality, thanks to the inextinguishable flame of the sense of self and dignity of man referred somewhere above.

Though modern media put all the efforts to show contemporary world as open, transparent and egalitarian under capitalistic-democratic order, the never ending bloody wars for capturing state power in every corner of the world that we have seen in the beginning of this write-up exposes the lie.

Modern world must find out better models of egalitarianism, freedom and individual dignity, to end the above serious malady of this age. Some models are suggested at our
blogs: http://whatequalityshouldmeanindemocracy.blogspot.in/, http://democracywithoutpoliticalparties.blogspot.in/2010/11/model-of-democracy-without-political.html etc.

A possible different story on the origin of the first establishment in the world can be seen at link: http://originofestablishment.blogspot.in/

Please visit following link to see about the great vacuum in the world for a new philosophy of life: http://newphilosophyoflife.blogspot.in/

Article-7

Politics: Danger of its excessive permeation into every aspect of modern life

(OR) World turning a 'political market', ending its tryst with 'civil society'

After the end of the widespread European colonization, one could say, world has turned a large civil society. There were strong signals of civic-rights emanating from every corner. Undiluted rights and liberty of men was the prime target of every modern government. Political institutions were supposed to be mere means and instruments towards achieving the above universal goal of modern societies. It seemed that individual citizen in the world has finally became the King !

This brief post is aimed at re-examining the current status of the reign of individual citizen in the contemporary world.

Though democracy was the most sacred thing that human civilization has contributed towards making the individual man the King in civil societies, it took dramatic turns and twists in its course of development after the American revolution. America was the first modern state that had thought of experimenting with the old sacred system of the government of the 'people', after its ancient reign in Greece and some other parts of the world.

The experiment was nothing short of a ' wonder' for the modern world, which was struggling to gain some political stability after the end of the long hegemony of the Church, and the emergence of many 'nation states'. French government sent its envoy, a young Judicial officer- Alexis De.Tocqueville- to America to personally report back as to what the new system was, and how does it work. Tocqueville's book ' Democracy in America' is one of the monumental work on this experiment. He was in all praise of the new wonder system.
In one of the instances of his such praises, he says at page-256:

' However irksome an enactment of (law) may be, the citizen of the United States complies with it, not only because it is the work of the majority, but because it is his own, and he regards it is a contract to which he is a party'.

The central thrust of the new peoples' form of government was to 'restrict' the powers of the government from exploiting the rights of people than its elaborate clauses and arrangement to impose its authority over the citizens.

The origin of the political party system in America that marked the end of 'people oriented' democracy

In the later years of American Democracy, Thomas Jefferson and Hamilton had great difference of opinion about the economic direction of the government; ie. whether to nurture big industry in the country or to be happy with the smaller ones. Whether to be a highly industrialized nation, or to remain as an agrarian nation. There started USA's existing two party political system, the Republicans and the Democrats. How this chance accident in the history of America had caused to alter the very face of Democracy is plain history before every one of us.

Politics has taken birth as a highly professional activity of a section of the people. The divide of a virgin people on the economic direction of their country had later got transformed into multiple divisions on various other causes such as geographic region and language, religion, caste and creed, peace and revolution, and what not. The political advantage of having multiple divisions in the country has taken predominance over the real ideological 'cause' of such divisions.

When these modern governments turned more and more 'economic' entities than 'rights' entities of people, thanks to the central role played by the new industrial class in bringing 'development' into these countries, 'politics' has become the chief theme of modern states than democracy. Politics here mean the art and science of winning elections and forming governments based on the principle of majority. Welfare and Rights oriented democracy had to give way for 'power' and 'development' oriented democracy. People centred democracy of old America has transformed into 'politics' centred democracy all over the world.

For the purpose of the newly evolved concept of 'development', states had to depend more and more on the new industrial class for opening more and more factories. Thus industry has become the integral backbone of every nation in the world. **Success of a state started to be measured on the size of its economy.** The class of industrialists in every nation ceased to exist as mere people, but integral partners in running of modern states. Laws and budgets were made more for keeping the interest of the industrialists and traders safe than for ensuring the rights and welfare of the people of the country.

Having a friendly government at the helm of affairs has become the central necessity of the industrial class. Without a friendly government, running of any industry has became an impossible proposition, chiefly due to the fear of **antagonistic licence and taxation laws**. Thus, politics has gradually turned the central theme of modern democracy, and democracy meant just an old model POWER-STATES now its seats occupied by members from the peoples class !

Relevance of Election has become central, as it involved the fate of thousands and thousands of industrial houses in every country. Therefore, every industrial house kept special budget allocation for meeting election expenses in the country. The exercise of winning elections has become a gigantic marketing and propaganda exercise and task in every democratic nation. It involved large quantities of money, meticulous planning and strategizing, elaborate technological aids like electronic communication and display techniques, best managerial and communication skills and what not !

Unlike the usual marketing methods of commercial products, winning elections in modern democracies has become an extremely sophisticated exercise, needing special experience and expertise in reading and predicting the mind and behaviour of voters, choosing of special agendas and planks for wooing people, selecting propaganda teams to cover the entire country, intelligence network to spy the opponents' strategies and plans etc.etc. After the elaborate use of electronic communication and image-building technologies in the last US election, some political leaders in India also have adopted them successfully at home. The usage of 3G technology by Narendra Modi, the former Gujrat state Chief minister, (Now PM of India) in remote transmitting of his image and speech to distant States and locations during elections deserves special mention here to exemplify this latest tendency.

The irresistible power of the expressed word and images is a well proven fact in the world. Whatever is repeatedly bombarded into the human mind definitely enters there, and stay there. **This factor throws serious shadow on the 'free-choice' myth of country's voters** ! He is a poor victim of the effective use of powerful electronic propaganda devices and techniques available with the political players !

Whatever we have seen and discussed above help the open minds to infer that modern political system has turned contemporary world into a 'political market place'. It is an open battlefield of political entities to capture supremacy in the market.

While mankind can not write-off the social and political need of a 'representative government' to get individual's rights defined and established, contemporary world can not also ignore the dangerous turning of such sacred realms of public into plain battlefields to capture such realms, for the sake of its hidden power and other agendas. It is an urgent need of the world to open its eyes towards the above observed dangerous twists and turns at its political realm.

Article -8

Modern notion of State: 'means' usurping the 'end' !

Modern States show tendency to zombiefy the people !

The recent demise of the father figure of Singapore, Lee Kuan Yew, has seen many world leaders as well as popular media columnists coming-out with unprecedented adulation and appreciation about him, and the way he enhanced the reputation of his small nation, by his sheer mastery over the so called ' State-Craft' !

He could achieve the said envious feat by following certain key strategies that every nation-head is keen to emulate:
1) Not allowing the political opponents to come-out strong, and stand in his way of bringing in progress and modernity ('suppression of political dissent' as stated by Minxin Pei, prof. of govt.at Claremont McKenna college,US, in his article in Indian Express, dated 30th March,2015)
2) His model of dynamic, authoritarian capitalism (words of same author as above, in the same article)

3) A market-based economy, closely integrated with the West (-do-)

4) A strategic alliance with US (-do-)

One of the most respected voices among the Indian political and policy analysts Mr. Bhanu Pratap Mehta, President of Center of policy Research, also wrote an article in Indian Express Newspaper last week, a distinctly adulatory piccc on the overall performance of the Late. Lee Kuan Yew !

If one attempt to summarize the many such highly praising accounts of the achievements of the late great leader of Singapore, it comes-out that, what modern world count and respect is the PROGRESS of countries as a stand-alone goal, irrespective, and **independent** of what and how individual citizens subjectively experience the said concept of success and progress! The State is the entity and the 'being' that glitter, shine, compete, and compare itself with other nations over the criteria of 'success' and 'progress' listed above.

It would be similar to large cattle-farm owners, comparing and competing with each other, about production, profitability and professional working-model of their farms ! Animals in the farm are mere passive instruments and means for the farms to be successful and outshining over others ! What, after-all, is the relevance of the individual animals in the farm, other than that of the owners meeting their biological needs ? Animals are mere 'means' or commodity in the farm-owners' professional line of activity ! Or, for another comparison, we could do it with the motivation of a Gardner; a gardener is more concerned with the beauty of the 'clusters' he grooms, than the breathing space of each individual plant. The 'collective' picture is his concern always, than nurturing individual plants.

Is it not a very dangerous outlook on the life of man on planet earth ? Considering the citizens only at their physical level dimension and needs, at the heavy cost of NOT taking into consideration each citizen's overall intellectual, emotional, rational and creative needs? After-all, he is the one who ultimately 'experience' the net quality of life that the state produce, and such quality is definitely NOT confined around physical factors alone. Human person is primarily and ultimately an emotional and 'mind' thing, for whom the question of his individual, creative self-expression is central for his contentment and happiness.

If every budding and ambitious new leader of nations attempt to emulate the great Singapore leader,
(without doubt, these leaders are extremely desirous of being like him in the matter of state-craft and SUCCESS !) what will the future of mankind as an enlightened species ?

Modern democratic State were supposed to be a mere 'means' to ensure individual freedom, dignity of self, and liberty from the exploitation of the powerful over the weak, as well from, and most importantly, by the State itself. While this remains the cardinal principle of the democratic ideal, emulating Late. Lee of Singapore by every modern world leader will be a great ideological catastrophe for the future of mankind !

Increasingly, the realm of people is being treated as passive material for the existence of the primary entity of the State, and to glorify its existence as once stated above.

The end goal of all modern states was people, post the enlightenment era. But in the unfortunate developments that occurred with the reign of industry in modern world, this exalted status of man in the scheme of things drastically altered. Man's subjective entity, his contentment as individual has lost its centrality in the modern world. As stated once, the chief cause behind this vital shift of centrality was the unprecedented entry of industry and professional politics in the mainstream world.

The post-industrial world wanted all its men as chief resource to run factories and offices. Modern political democracies, by default under the modern-economic myths and traditions, happened to be depended upon the industry for achieving 'progress' of their respective nations. We know that, the imperial colonization by the European powers had happened only as a natural follow-up act; whatever the individual trade and business adventurers and players had achieved was appropriated by the respective European governments in due course of history. Best example is the East India Company, a private trading establishment in Britain. They traveled to India and established their huge trade as well as military hold in India. When almost the entire geographic region of India was under the said private-player, the Queen of England had appropriated the Indian-holdings of the company by an Act in parliament in 1958. This tradition of industry and ruling establishment going hand-in-hand is being continued even today also, without much change.

The above stark-reality about the status of human-beings, and their centrality in the affairs of modern world should send moral and rational tremors through the spine of every right-thinking person ! Though there already exists, and then regularly appear huge literature and out-cries about the ever-losing rights and individual centrality of man in the media, such literature are merely becoming permanent and even DECORATIVE feature of modern-mainstream ! They make no difference to the well-cemented norms, systems and traditions of modern world, where individual-freedom has become the most scarce but precious commodity today; becoming either rich or politically powerful are the only two means to grab and possess it!

The above referred utter scarcity of human-freedom, and the wide-spread violent scramble for political power at every corner of modern world amply exemplify the above proposition; the currently hot events in Yemen, wherein the Houthis from the Shia-camp wanted to capture power and be free. In Nigeria, the Boko-Haram rebels wanted to capture power and be free from the current establishment. In India, it is said, in almost 30% of districts in the country, the anti-government groups(seeking freedom!) like Maoists are active. Those who get to the seats of political power, by whatever method, they fail or simply refuse to ensure and share the much prized human-freedom to all the people! It is high-time for modern world to sit for long, and debate the appropriateness and relevance of SUCCESS and DEVELOPMENT, over providing uninhibited and plain individual liberty and freedom to each citizen !

It is easy to understand restricted individual freedom and liberty under regimes of Kings and tyrants. But the same restrictions and limitations under Democracy, the so called political system of EQUAL-MEN is pure-self-deception over the great ideal !

It is high-time for mankind as a whole to realize that, the most archaic and primeval notion,or we could say, the social-evil that contemporary world lives with is its notions about the realm of State, or Establishment ! Despite all the progress and advancement she claims, modern world is still in the grip of primitive notions about how our societies are ruled. The realm of State and country RULE is still clouded under old-time myths of glitter, glory and power. Therefore, dangerous clamors in every state is a reality, between different groups to capture these excessively glorified THRONES ! That between different nations in the world, each State accumulating planet-threatening modern nuclear-weaponry should shame every aspect of our claiming as a modern age !

For our becoming truly modern, open and progressive, we must alter our basic concepts, myths, notions and values around our realm of RULING the states ! These myths and notions are archaic and primitive to the tilt!

For further reading on the above subject, please follow these links:
http://closedmodernworlddespitedemocracy.blogspot.in/
http://influxofcapitalisticvalues.blogspot.in/
http://understandinginflationinanewlight.blogspot.in/2014/12/freedom-and-free-market-are-they.html

----

Article-09

Are modern democratic-capitalistic societies closed, RIGHTIST dungeons ?

(or) The stark similarity of all right-wing ideologies; whether it is religious, political or economic

One could easily identify and classify the traits of right-wing groups in all sectors of life; religion, politics, and even in economics. As the meaning and correct distinction of right wing ideology in economic field is not yet clearly identified in the modern world, this is an attempt to identify this distinct trait, and also to observe its disturbing, all engrossing grip over all other segments of life.

Right-wing, or rightist ideology has a distinct social model, as to what kind of a human society they idealize with regard to the treatment towards, or the status of the 'outsider' in any society; whether in religion, political, or economic field. All of them believe in the superiority of their sect, or class. They do not believe in the equality of all human beings in the world, or that of every living beings in existence.

On close scrutiny, one could observe that every human being was ' rightist' when he was leading his primeval life in jungle. Every man had shared the animal ideology of self-centeredness during the jungle time. Civilization was exclusively the route and means to get these jungle creatures transformed into human beings, and to civil, or civilized ways, that included chiefly mending of his ways with his fellow beings. But even after the pinnacle of our modern civilization, it would be sad and extremely disturbing to NOTICE that, what we have as civilization and progress today is the highly institutionalized ways of the right wing political and economic ideologists ! What they follow is a path of extreme exclusion, aiming at the flourishing of only a select few, or at least they are not interested in any kind of universal advancement of mankind in general. For them, such ideals are waste of time and efforts.

An open minded observer could attribute even the tendency of male gender to feel superior over the female gender also, to the same RIGHTIST mind-set. It is probably the primeval urge of the ego to keep everything around it in its control, as it could not grasp the existence of anything other than itself, real !

Let us look deeper into this calamity, and understand its hidden dynamics.

Freedom was always a concept for a select few, even during the inception stage of such concepts !

Modern world now know very clearly that during the inception stage of democracy in old Greece, the citizenship was limited among the land owning minority. Even when it was introduced in USA in the modern era, it took many years to get it introduced to universal suffrage, ie. the right to vote for women and the slaves.

When the notions of LIBERALISM was widely spread in Europe post enlightenment, it was basically the unlimited freedom for the 'gentlemen' class of the time for whom it was really envisaged for. It comprised of the new class of Nobles, now totally free from the supremacy of the Royal class, as well as from the authority of the Church. Industrial revolution and the subsequent adventurous travels to exotic foreign lands, searching for new markets and raw materials was basically undertaken by this class, or at least financed by this class.

All the freedom that this age had sought was basically for this privileged class of human beings! Like the narrow sense about suffrage, the purview of freedom and liberty also was envisaged for, or restricted to this select class of people. If the citizenship in nations was limited to a select few, how can the definition of mankind could be inclusive of the entire population of earth ?

The men who worked in the factories, and who assisted these free men in their freedom-march was the majority element in the society, ie. common men in European nations. They were always the passive 'subjects' in the nations that constituted the **'people material'** for every modern democratic nation.

Except probably in the early America, in most of the early Europe, the above story was true. In America, every citizen had hailed from an equal back-ground, and the disparity occurred only after many years of its unequal economic development.

The newly found liberty and freedom was only meant for the cream in the new society. After the onset of industrial revolution, the common artisans, and the small farmers and farm workers were lured into the factories as workers. These large scale working class was what formed the **new middle class** of today, in every modern nation.

To understand clearly the phenomenon that we discuss here, ie. the transformation of old liberalistic ideas into later stage 'Laissez-faire' capitalism, and the building up of modern economy into a RIGHT-WING social reality, we must look at the similar fate happened with communism too. Communism was born out from the great empathy felt by Karl Marx with sufferings of the European labour class in the then multitude of factories. But when his well meant ideology had got translated into political communism in Russia and later in China, it too had turned into a rightist kind of phenomenon with regard to its attitude towards other classes in society, and towards all 'outsiders' to their ideology.(the 'class enemies' in the communist terminology) It has terribly failed to evolve as an all 'inclusive', humanitarian alternative to Capitalism. Every class or sect who gained political power in their hands always turned RIGHTISTS in attitude and ideology, as it involved OWNERSHIP of what they had already gained, or what was in their possession !

The communist leadership ultimately had become just like their one time tormentors- the capitalists- in substance and spirit. They grew equally intolerant towards the opposite economic and social classes, ending the hope of the world for a healthy alternative to capitalism. As we have seen above, rightist ideology was always characterized by such total intolerance towards other classes, sects and groups.

Susan George, a fiery activist against the Neo-liberalism of modern age has said:

" I submit that neo-liberalism has changed the fundamental nature of politics.

Politics used to be primarily about who ruled whom and who got what share of the pie. Aspects of both these central questions remain, of course, but the great new central question of politics is, in my view, **"Who has a right to live and who does not"**. Radical exclusion is now the order of the day, I mean this deadly seriously". (in her paper presented at Conference on Economic Sovereignty in a Globalizing World,Bangkok, 24-26 March 1999)

How does the economic rightist ideology now rule the world ?

Liberalism, and its later development into the economic system of capitalism, was basically stood on the principles of unhindered freedom for individual growth, and his unbound creativity. When I seek such unhindered freedom for myself, and if I do not develop a fitting philosophy for allowing the same degree of freedom for my fellow beings too, it would naturally bump into serious social and philosophical problems, especially when the sacred principle had got translated into a distinct economic system- Capitalism.

Capitalism is all about ownership. Ownership in every form generates gigantic existential issues and crises, centered around the need to protect and maintain the ownership. All past wars were around protecting one's country from enemies, or expanding the 'ownership' of one's existing country. In the animal Kingdom, whether it is large animals like lions and elephants, or the small counterparts like insects, the ownership wars over one's harems and territories are well known ! One's assets are strict extensions of one's existential self, whether it is own country, own capitalistic investment, or own harem of females ! Ownership presents grave existential problems to every living entity ! Here the old liberalists HAD TO turn protagonist of one's own freedom, or that of his group, or class. There was NO viable alternative.

Safeguarding one's own unrestricted freedom, and at the same time safeguarding it for the entire society in an institutional set-up, or as a social ideal, was an extremely difficult existential task ! **The very process of civilization was basically meant to find a solution for this existential issue; to get the above 'natural'(animal) trait of man transformed into that of a new being, a social, or civil being !** To have one's unbound freedom without minding that of all others around, will always pose grave social tension and imbalance.

It is here that capitalism, and its liberalistic bottom ideas had degenerated into the present purely RIGHTIST modern capitalist-democratic socio-political system.

One would wonder from where does this DEMOCRATIC link has descended on capitalism, partnering rightist ideology. Let us try to find out.

The development of nations has become exclusively economic development after the industrial revolution

The death of Church in Europe was the end of the anything spiritual in the world, and the start of the reign of the spirit of man. Science gained the role of the new Church, with its reign over the minds of man, his political as well as economic systems.

The highly enthused entrepreneur class, representing the new spirit of the age, conquered the entire world. They became the new 'providers' in mankind for their food, and every other daily needs for making life a splendid experience than never before. The fast transport systems, the new telecommunication system, weather control devises, wonder medicines etc. were more than what man had ever expected from life ! Science could effortlessly oust God from the entire realm of life.

Modern nations, mostly now run by peoples representatives, had no option but to adopt the same paradigm of development in their nations that the industry had introduced. The chief slogans around inalienable rights of man (and associated slogans of FREEDOM and LIBERTY) that arose with the American and French revolutions has given away for a **development** on the above lines. Roads, airports and factories have become the new symbols of development. Any government who could ensure these development symbols was known as successful.

Naturally, these democratic governments, earlier led by the highly principled ideologies for human freedom and dignity, had to give away the seats of power to the new breed of professional Political men and groups, who could successfully work with these new saviors of the world- the industrial houses ! No time was required for the development of a dangerous collusion between these new political professionals and the industrialists for working for the common goal- the development of their respective nations ! Both groups sought each other for safeguarding own agenda and goal.

Democracy, an ideal which was NOT clearly defined or identified on its fundamental principles except that it is a system of having country rulers from the REALM of PEOPLE, started having a rush of men and groups to fill this grandeur vacuum of the celebrated and mythological REALM OF THE COUNTRY RULERS ! NO other qualification, or norm of being a democratic RULER was ever established, for want of ideas and concepts for the new realm. Hence, in most of the nations in Europe as well as in USA, such governments took charge, and all these nations attained DEVELOPMENT of the sort that mentioned earlier. The rest of the world looked at Europe with awe and envy !

The industrialists had their firm voice in the running of governments, as the entire nation depended upon their entrepreneur-skills for country development. The norm of life and politics in the world got set on these arrangement.

The new masters of society !

During the middle ages, the feudal Lords were the masters in society. Church authority was also there to share this mastery. For a short interim period of enlightenment, it was the reign of the uninhibited mind of man! Then, as seen in the above story, the mastery over the mind and lives of men was fallen into the hands of the new coalition; the capitalistic –democratic coalition ! **This did not happen out of any intentional conspiracy, but out of natural human tendency to grab any chance to have more freedom, and more control over the environment.**

The old peoples class, the eternal material for constituting any state, has become the same impersonal material for the new democratic governments too. Though now they started to enjoy better living conditions in the world, **their exclusion from the mainstream was absolute.** The entire world has become like a single gigantic work place, or factory ! The old scientific spirit of the 18th and 19th centuries, marked by the quest for knowledge, inquiry and freedom has died down long back. Such qualities were not at all required at the new work places. Professional industry management system runs on the cardinal principles of zero wastage, and maximized profit. Without absolute efficiency on these two aspects, no business is its names worth.

The business acumen of men has long replaced the old supremacy of warlords, and feudal-lords in society. Those who share this unique quality in society out-shined every other quality and propensity in life ! These men, along with their mentors and protectors in the political sector, have become the new masterly class in the contemporary world.

For every practical purpose, there is a clear exclusion of ordinary people from the mainstream world, run and controlled by the money of the capitalists, and the political power of the democratic leaders. The former are needed only as workers and officers in the factories of the industrialists, and as party workers and voters by the political class. Their role in society is fixed. Any one crossing the well marked boundary is marked, caught, and ousted by the former, and caught and jailed by the latter.

Well imagined signs and symbols of an open world are abundant, like the so called 'free' media, entertainment centers like cinema halls, malls and other recreation centers. All of them are owned by the same industrial houses, or are run in secret collaboration with the political men and groups, hence all the money spent by the people class gets back to the same coffers.

Media houses are also mostly run by the same industry-politician nexus. Hence, they create mental images that are absolutely fit for the subdued class of people, through their projecting the world, men and events 24 hours a day.

An important special sign of the current right-wing economic and political realm is the open entry system. **Anyone can get into the new money making ways of the contemporary world,** and join the controlling group. They, without exception, get all the exclusive respect and privileges reserved for the money-power class in the modern world ! There isn't any discrimination in this respect, as was there for entry into the dominant class/group in olden times.

Then they share all other well known traits of other rightist sects; like the disdain for those who are not as bright as them in business acumen and entrepreneurship skills, not as equal to them in wealth and standard of living, not having any share in the political power and authority etc. The realm of common citizens is very carefully set apart, and any crossing of the line of control is severely dealt with. If it is in the work-place, such freedom seeker, or any one who shows tendency for questioning the authority is immediately thrown out ! If it is against the government and establishment, it would be definitely police, tax or municipal harassment, and if possible arrest and jail term.

A whole lot of human-beings are thrown out of the mainstream society every day in this manner, disdained and neglected, discarded and psychically maimed ! These men, totally lost their sense of dignified selves, have turned nothing like except brutes of the jungle ! One who lost his self-hood cannot ever treat the other human-being with dignity and regard. How can I treat you unlike others have treated me ? So, these identity lost men are the bane of modern society; they rape, they kill, they set-fire to neighbour's houses at times of communal tensions, they have no respect for morals and social-laws, they fall easy-prey to the calls for joining terrorist organizations... (these organizations too initiated by the soul-lost men of our unfortunate
age !) Every single advantage of modern age and its so called prosperity is marred by the default-generation of thousands of such men every-day at every corner of modern world,and the peace and security of the lives of men, and their social and political institutions.

Calling heinous acts of these unfortunate men as sin against humanity, and book/jail and hang-them is most ridiculous acts, as modern society has made these men sick and neurotic ! They are deprived of their right-mindedness and sanity, inherent qualities of human-race !

An open realm of mind is totally absent. Genuine thoughts and ideas are never encouraged, as, such activities without any CASH VALUE have no relevance, or use in strict economic sense. Realm of ideas and mind always has the upper hand of media veterans, top industrialists and popular political leaders, or such writers and sports-icons who are in the good books of the establishment.

Political realm takes all the care for NOT allowing outsiders to creep into the party inner circles. Strict hierarchical traditions are always maintained to ensure loyalty towards the leadership.

Thus, though it is not in the open awareness of the main-stream of modern age, it lives under the same kind of full fledged RIGHTIST society, especially in its democratic-capitalistic pockets ! The only pity is that while man is well aware and cautious about a real Rightist society, this particular calamity is hidden from public awareness. It flourishes under the guise of OPENNESS and TRANSPARENCY, thanks for having modern media as a close partner in the deal..

Why an open society is not feasible under power oriented modern democratic establishments ?

When the other person represents institutionalized power of any sort, I could only be either his boot licker/sycophant, or a plain collaborator in the execution of his power ! When a society is laden with such power holding individuals, such society can not be an open society, because no one would really be able to express his or her creativity or individuality uninhibited. Conformity, and always wait for orders from up would be the most safe options in such societies.

Power has this damaging tendency to cripple open thought. It gets shared with great enthusiasm deep down wards, covering every point of free human activity. Life simply gets reduced to one or the other of the above two divisions, and nothing else !

Modern day democracy suffers from this great calamity the most. It has got reduced to an intellectual self-deception due to the institutionalized political power it still holds at its central arenas. Though democracy has an image of openness around it, due to the existence of real political and institutionalized power at its centre, the air of openness always turns a farce !

Democracy should have devised a governance system truly compatible with the needs of a government of equal men at its inception stage itself. Unfortunately, there was no such model available in history at any point of time. Hence, the old governmental system and its power oriented governance machinery got inherited by democracy too. The myth and the institution of governmental power had remained with the peoples form of government too, till this date. Hence, mankind failed to develop into truly open societies under modern democracy too.

The elected ministers and parliamentarians enjoy governmental power in the same degree that the old time kings had enjoyed once. The natural brotherhood that shared by the the power-holders, thanks to the perennial fear of the power holders about its potential threat from the freedom seekers, has resulted into its dangerous consolidation at every point of country governance. Its wide spread sharing in the government machinery, from the ministers to the bureaucrats, then to the police officers and tax collectors, municipal officials, its drivers and even attendants has succeeded in making democracy a real farce in the modern world. **Individual turns not only a victim, but rather a helpless prey in modern democracies !**

Though individual freedom is said to be the hallmark of democracy, he has become the most vulnerable item under it. **What every government servant represents is the massive, dark power of the establishment.** Due to the above seen natural brotherhood among the power holders, anyone even slightly showing resentment against authority would be branded as a threat to THEIR society ! As seen above, majority of men helplessly join the show either as sycophant, or a collaborating partner, thus totally isolating the remaining miniscule free-minded individuals. Self-survival becomes the key priority in such societies. Being with the system as an obliging member becomes the only available success mantra. Instead of pure life thriving, it becomes a dreadful drag for every man !.

Media's devastating role in showing the system as open !

At some unfortunate point in the history of modern democracy, media was pictured as a sign of the openness and transparency of our societies. They represent the FREEDOM OF SPEECH of the citizens !

As earlier seen, only two roles are possible under any power oriented establishment; either that of a sycophant, or a collaborating partner. Like a physical law, freedom seekers can only be potential threats in such societies. Hence, media naturally had no other option but to be collaborating partners in the system. But they were compelled to wear the mask of freedom seekers, as the traditional role they were supposed to occupy was that of 'peoples voice' and ' watch-dogs' in democracy. So, they sing songs of individual dignity and freedom every day, and play the double role of being with the people and the power holding establishment ! While such a media is in existence, no one would be able to raise the neck, and cry about non-freedom Thus media is the smart cover up agent in every democratic government in the modern world. They smartly suppress the truth that modern democracy is nothing different to people than the old regimes of Kings and foreign rulers. The fierceness of the institutionalized power of the establishment is no less severe under modern democracies, or it is worse due to its multiples power holding agents present at every point of man's day to day life !

<u>Why open societies fail to evolve in the contemporary world ?</u>

The existing political systems are so authoritarian that every human being, irrespective of he being a politician, an industrialist or a common man, is neurotically anxious to keep his individuality and free-self safe. As no existing political system is successful in offering universal sense of freedom to all, each one try to care only for his own freedom, adjusting oneself the most successful way in the existing rot, and keep his head above the water. This is similar to the old jungle atmosphere, wherein everyone turns against everyone else, purely for survival.

Besides the state-authority centered political establishment - Capitalism - the reigning economic system-also has contributed much towards diminishing the contemporary world into a highly hierarchical power system. The rich and the resourceful enjoy an untold supremacy in society. This class, who inevitably keep their links with the political counterparts for safe running of their enterprises, adds up to the misery of the less resourceful and the common folk. If it was merely a difference in the quality of food one eats and the type of cloth one wear, or the size of the dwelling unit one lives in, things would have been quite acceptable. These are natural inequality like the size and shape of one's body. **The problem is with the difference in the degree of DIGNITY the lesser individuals enjoy in the mainstream society ! They face despise and disregard in every walk of life ! It makes this class feel marginalized, and out from the mainstream.** These marginalized human selves act like agitated subatomic particles that have escaped from their orbits, struggling to break free from the organized norms of society. It naturally lead them into deviant behavior and criminality. They are entities with lost selves ! Modern world, with it deceptive democracy and ever increasing grip of capitalism, witness these negatively charged human beings gushing out in large numbers every day into our cities and villages, in every country ! They are unconnected, free and dangerous. They don't care to rob, kill, rape, and easily become available for terrorist activities. This counter reaction to the modern development paradigm in the modern world nullify all its much acclaimed achievements and grandeur !

If media adopt itself to the role of true 'peoples voice' and expose the above dangers, public awareness would develop, and society as a whole would thrive to workout and evolve fresh social systems with universal freedom as its goal. If they can not directly take up this role, they could at least let men of mind to express these ideals through their medium in a life changing tone. Absence of any agency in the modern world to stand for such causes, especially the DOGMATIC media that do not accept this role, is the root cause of the darkness in the contemporary world !

The utter need of evolving new myths and models of a new democracy

Like an outdated religious dogma, democracy revolves around its few known symbols; elections and the existence of media. The spirit and substance of the ideal has gone back to oblivion. The society as a whole must sit-down and debate what the life of men should be like, under a true peoples form of government, a governance system of equal men. Such a need should devise and define the necessary means for achieving the set goals . Democracy has today degenerated into an old belief system, with least touch with its intended need, purposes and goals.

Article-10

Why modern societies deliberately create avenues of inequality ?

There are outcries from every sector in modern world about ever growing inequality. Every study by reputed institutions reveals that more and more wealth and privileges are going into fewer and fewer hands, and the number of poor and unprivileged human-beings are ever increasing in the world. The recent Oxfam study and Zurich study are examples.

The recent post by Bill Gates in the Linkedin PULSE column (see link: https://www.linkedin.com/pulse/article/20141015002149-251749025-why-inequality-matters?trk=prof-post) commenting on Thomas Piketty's book on Capital, also acknowledges that inequality in the capitalist order is a naked reality. He suggested to tax increasingly on consumption, instead of the existing practice of taxing income to achieve more effective economic equality.

This is an attempt to get at the root fundamentals of inequality in modern societies. Some of the basic questions raised here to achieve this end are:

1) Is inequality a simple issue of unequal wealth distribution in society ?

2) What aspect of inequality pains the victim most;

a) Having lesser wealth or income than the more privileged ?

b) The capacity of the wealthy to enjoy all the luxuries of the world, depriving them from the common folk ?

c) His irrelevance in the society that is primarily measured on the basis of what one does to earn his bread, (his job, or earning source) the attire and foot-wear he uses, where does he live,(the status of the colony /street he resides) the brand of car he uses, the style of language he uses (the degree of sophistication of his language) etc?

3) Does one's power-share in the polity also strongly contribute to inequality ? In other words, other than income disparity, does power-disparity also cause grave inequality ?

4) Is there a definite striving in modern society to always become unequal? (to be above the common)

5) Does our existing socio-economic-political system directly or indirectly encourages a striving for becoming more and more wealthy and successful in society ? The naked reality of economic-class distinction measured and relished on the basic of the 'class', or the 'luxury' standards of the products and services one could afford to go for...

6) Is it not paradoxical for the modern world that at one hand it strives for equality as a socio-political value, and at the same time it encourages men and women to compete, and attain unequal heights in society ?
Let us take-up the above 6 points one by one here, for quick discussions on each question:

1) Is inequality a simple issue of unequal wealth distribution in society ?
The answer is a plain NO ! The poorest who dwells in an urban labor-hut but eats his 3 square-meals every day in his own tradition and style, does not bother if the extreme-rich does the same act, with an entirely different menu on his plate, and

having the affair on a dining table costing many fortunes that the poor man can ever think of. For both the specimen, it is only a matter of inherited tastes and routines. If healthy, both models sleep well after having dinner, having some fun with the children, and then after a routine sex act ! Both parties live their lives, unaware of how the other one undergoes his life. They virtually live in two different worlds !

So, their lives are not qualitatively any different on account of the huge income/wealth difference .Here, quality of life standard is measured on the basis of the degree of contentment both models have; not based on any objective, external criterion. Issue of inequality does not at all bother them at this plane of life.

2) What aspect of inequality pains the victim most;

a) Having lesser wealth or income than the more privileged ? (the deprivation aspect)

We could simply compare this factor with men and women with lesser body length. Except in very rare cases, body height does not affect one's base-line happiness in life. We can not ever conclude that the more the body length of a person, the higher would be his contentment in life, and the lesser it, the lesser his/her degree of happiness. As far as one has resources for 3 square meals and a roof to sleep under, the different way in which the other eat, drink or sleep will not disturb anyone's base-line happiness.

The cases of extreme poverty, ie. one's going to bed with out having anything to eat is an extremely rare event in the modern world, with many charitable and religious institutions who routinely offer food every day to those who come calling (The Sikh temples, for example)

b) The capacity of the wealthy to enjoy all the luxuries of the world, depriving them from common folk ?
Some of the explanations above would answer this question; many in the lower strata of modern societies are even not aware what the rich eats, the luxury gadgets he uses at home. The two worlds are quite set-apart, and the inherited

style and routine, rules their food and life habits than any sense of constant deprivation, or injustice.

c) His irrelevance in the society that is predominantly measured on the basis of what one does (his job and earning source) the attire and foot-wear he uses, where does he live,(the size of his house, status of the colony /street he resides) the brand of car he uses, the style of language he utters (his education and the life-style ladder!) etc?

Yes...other than the food he eat, or the kind of roof he sleeps under, or the dress he wears, what disturbs the poor and down-trodden most is the distinct and clear low-status in which the main-stream world look-upon and treat him!

There are clear mental divisions in society, or class distinctions, that determine one's status and relevance in the society, measured on the basis of his social appearance. When such distinct divisions exist, and when people get corresponding response from the society in the form of respect and regard for his status, every person is compelled to internalize his/her such 'allotted' dignity and value in the society, and adjust his himself, his looks and behavior accordingly.

He wears a fitting self-image, many a times that of a dangerous self-hatred and self-denial ! He renounce the world that disparage him. He self-declares his non-belonging-ness to such a world, and create his own separate a world to dwells in. For any healthy society, such alienation of a percentage of the population into their own world of negative values and self-image is an extremely dangerous feature ! They are the ones who could disturb the very bottom peace in any society, by their criminal, terrorist or plain underworld activities, nullifying whatever is splendid and extra-ordinary about an age ! Our contemporary age's socio-political condition is a fitting example !

In short, the inequality as sensed by these men in the bottom strata of society is not based on his income or wealth inequality, but his degree of dignity and relevance the society offer him. It is about the class into which he is dumped, as an inevitable feature of the economic and political ways of the existing order.

3) Does one's power-share in the polity also strongly contribute to inequality ? In other words, other than income disparity, does power-disparity also cause grave inequality ?

This might be a rarely taken-up cause, or a feature of modern inequality. Modern democracy is simply a political power-sharing exercise among certain professional class of people. Every conceivable group in society, ie. religious, language, geography and even certain occupation like farmers are in a mad rush to form political parties, fight election, and have a participation in the government. Unrepresented groups and individuals often left alone in modern democracies, without power and any influence in the decision making process. This often leads to grave issues of inequality in society.

There are thousands of bureaucrats under every government, with the whole backing of the state, and a power-share in it. A good percentage of population are friends and relatives of these men, with equal hold in the power-basket, and they too do enjoy unlimited freedom and equality in society.

The rest multitudes are left alone, as mere power-less 'subjects' in the country. In the matter of being 'heard', or getting routine citizens matters done in govt. offices, or for gaining freedom from police, taxation, and municipality highhandedness, ordinary citizens routinely have to either bribe, or plead mercy from the ones in power for personal safety and survival. The snow-balling effect is true in the mater of political power too, hence money and resources get attracted to political power, and **these guys increasingly grow very unequal in every modern democratic society.**

The general inequality and powerless-ness of common citizens has a lot to do with the above unequal distribution of political power. Those who are without any political link often get despised and ignored at government offices for routine work, and similarly at police, taxation and municipal offices. The ones with some or other kind of political 'power' (or even with money power, that always attracts political power) are **not a single individual in the strict sense of it; they are kind of monsters**, with the backing of a hugely powerful and impersonal entity called the State ! An individual citizen is no match for him, with his total vulnerability and defenselessness ! This inequality is, if analyzed carefully, is the worst form of inequality in the modern world.

4) Is there a definite striving in modern society to become unequal? (to be above the common)

We can answer only in the affirmative ! Yes... every one of us want to be up and above from the other, in the degree of dignity and relevance in society ! **This striving is for avoiding the ignominy of being an ordinary citizen in the country!**

If the criterion that had decided this difference from others was mere physical strength in the primordial days, it was changed to knowledge about the 'other' world of spirits and Gods (the priestly class) later on in history, in the journey of mankind. Most of the civilization had periods of domination by the priestly class in their history.

Then It was followed by Feudalism, the upper-hand of men with large land holdings and the 'noble' ways they had dressed, spoken and lived. The so called democratic transition was in-fact a seeking of freedom and empowerment by the rich and noble class from the monarchs. The Magna-Carta treaty- the first of its kind in history-was indeed wrestled by the feudal lords from the kings !

It is said that the British monarchies were forced to recognize the House of 'commons', at the instigation of the House of Lords. Feudal Lords thought that such a step would reduce the power of the Kings in the long-run. The power and wealth of over-seas voyagers, and later the industrialists (who were mostly from the class of common people) blinded even the then feudal Lords. Heard that some of them were ready even to exchange their noble-titles for the exotic items these voyagers brought from strange lands !

In short, no revolution -seeking freedom and liberty in history - was ever led by common citizens, genuinely wanting to alter their 'state-subject' status. They were all planned and executed by those who had been already rich and the powerful, wanting to escape the atrocities of the king or his likes. If American revolution was led by the rich planters in the new continent, hugely helped and supported by the French and the Spanish (to avenge their defeat in the 7 year war with Britain !) the French revolution was known to have planned and executed by the secret societies of Jewish money lenders, predominantly based in Britain and Germany (see link: http://www.lovethetruth.com/books/pawns/03.htm)

Whatever the case and cause might have been, though feudalism had come to an end, a similar upper-hand of a new class- the men of business and trade-took over the reigns of modern world from its old masters in 17th and 18th centuries. Though the peoples' form of government -democracy-took over major parts of the world from the days of American democratic experiment, for the much needed and inevitable country development,(ie. economic development) the new political order and the men behind it, had no choice but to seek the active participation and collaboration of these new masters of the world! (ie. from the industry and the elite sector)

The human individual is free today to have his own ways, (the liberal order) whether it is about building up huge castles for himself and his family, owning air-crafts and ships, creating exclusive realms of luxury and life-conveniences for him and his men and women etc. This freedom of individual under the liberal spirit of the West, is an unquestioned norm in the contemporary, so called free-world, provided he, (the rich and elite) and the companies he own pay taxes in time !There are many special industries catering to the unique needs of the life-style of these class of people, who own more than 50% of of all the wealth of the world as per authentic, recent studies.

Then comes the second, third, fourth and fifth etc.categories or classes of men with wealth and life-style, beneath the above 1%, the most elite class. There are specialized industries, products and services that cater to the needs of each of such economic class in the modern world.

Our knowledge of human nature is still inadequate to infer why man is in a constant pursuit to out-smart his fellow-being in success and achievement ! But one thing is clear that, our collective moral imperative always warn us (the mankind) that, equality is a better social-condition than the ever growing inequality in society that the capitalistic order will always usher-in. Without doubt, the striving for up-man-ship is a clear feature that our modern society is suffering from, and what the contemporary capitalist-democratic order indeed supports and encourages.

World have clearly witnessed the same outcome from its communist experiments too; many centuries of their reign at many parts of the world had not resulted in providing citizens their much promised liberation, individual dignity and peace. The so called 'workers' class, when successful in occupying the chairs of the 'ruling-class' of the states, had no other model to adopt, than that of the their predecessors who once they had ousted from those seats ! Today, communist nations are notorious for their lack of individual freedom for people, and for their despotic ways with the people.

There is a strange kind of equality under communist order, but it is like the equality of many 'zeros', with no value and relevance to any one. State is the ultimate unit of progress, success and fame !

Thus, communism also shut the hopes of mankind in ushering a new era of universal acceptance of individual human dignity and freedom.
If communists had made citizens the 'commodity' that constitute the state, modern capitalistic-democracies made them commodities for the machinery of industry to run!

Modern democratic-political order always play supportive role for the industry, as they provide the life-blood to the nationhood. Though there is constant strife between the polity and the industry on the question of who is the master of affairs in modern world, such conflicts are always outside the realm of people. People are always passive victims and state-material, as they were always been in human history !

America, the strongest of all democracies in the modern world, though succeeded in suppressing the recent agitation of the 99% of the population alleging that their cause is to free the nation from the reign of the 1% elites, (The recent 'OCCUPY' wall-street etc.,agitations) it exemplify whatever we have discussed in the preceding para.

Thus, it is clear that every individual attempts to be smarter and successful than his fellow-being, while nations too suffer from the same disease. This age believes that competition is the only natural order, and it only would ensure survival ! Should this dogma be right ? Please share a link that explains a different story, at link::http://newphilosophyoflife.blogspot.in/

Susan George, a fiery activist against the new-liberalism of our era, in one of her papers writes:

"There is plenty of money sloshing around out there and a tiny fraction, a ridiculous, infinitesimal proportion of it would be enough to provide a decent life to every person on earth, to supply universal health and education, to clean up the environment and prevent further destruction to the planet, to close the North-South gap--at least according to the UNDP which calls for a paltry $40 billion a year. That, frankly, is peanuts " (In her paper presented at 'Conference on Economic Sovereignty in a Globalising World' Bangkok, 24-26 March 1999,see link:
file:///C:/Documents%20and%20Settings/Father/Desktop/A%20Short%20History%20of%20Neo-liberalism%20%20%20Global%20Exchange.html)

5) Does our existing socio-economic-political system directly or indirectly encourage the above value of striving for becoming more and more wealthy and successful ? The naked reality of economic-class distinction measured and relished, on the basic of the 'class' or 'luxury' standards of the life-style products and services one can afford to purchase.

We have seen an affirmative answer to this question at question No..3 above. One's wealth or affluence is not measured by his bank-balance or cash in the purse. It is always measured and graded according to the 'class' or luxury of the life-style products and services one is able to purchase and own. The basic inequality is also predominantly gets expressed in the above way.

It is simple; social equality is dangerously hampered when some class of men can afford to buy a high-end mansion, or own and drive a high-end car, (that costs sometimes 100 times more than the lowest category /model available in the market) and they are accepted in exclusive social-pockets meant for them. Then come a secondary, third, fourth and fifth categories of such products and services exclusively meant to be bought by some other class of men, with price and luxury ranges, un-affordable by vast majority of the population. These classes are able to express their high-end status in society by possessing a fit -range of luxury houses, cars, hotel stay, air-travel, medical facilities, foot-wear, clothing, food and beverages and every house -hold items of class and luxury !

This class range of products (brands) and services has a clear hierarchy of price and status in the contemporary world, and their possession or affordability is what determines one's economic class, and of-course his social status, value and acceptance in society ! As once mentioned in a paragraph above, there are special industries catering to the need of each economic class, bringing-up fitting brands and imaginary social-status to pamper the respective self-image of the target end-user ! Using their brand or service helps the customer to express his 'class' (or unequal status) in the society in a distinct manner.

If our age genuinely wish to usher in social-equality, they could do so by restricting by law, the production of consumer items including dwelling units beyond a certain cost-range.

Thus, dwelling units, cars, house-hold consumer items, clothing, foot-wear and thousands of such products and SERVICES (like hotel-stay, air and land travel, health-care services, banking, insurance etc.etc) should be manufactured and offered at qualities and prices that could be afforded even by the last layer of economic-class in the country !

It is quite possible as a real model, as well as a lasting social value; see the example of the Metro-Rail services (the tube rail service) in various countries - - -such services are open and affordable to every citizen without class distinction. The service is of standard quality, (with all coaches air-conditioned) that no economic class could allege it as below-par. (see our dedicated blog on the theme, at link: http://whatequalityshouldmeanindemocracy.blogspot.in/, and sub-links referred in the said main blog)

Every such product and service in the world should be of same standard, (while upholding and respecting the creative idea in-puts of deserving minds !) leaving no avenue for the rich to show of his separate class distinction. This step could be aided by restricting salary difference also to a certain level; the difference between highest drawn and the lowest drawn salary must be restricted by law. Such steps would never hamper the valued human spirit and creativity; rather its net quantum would increase, by the addition of it from many thousands of men whose such qualities had no avenue for expression in the past.

6) Is it not paradoxical for the modern world that, at one hand it strives for equality as a socio-political value, and at the same time it encourage men and women to compete, and attain unequal heights in society ?
No one with open disposition could refute this allegation ; while the entire world cry-out about inequality, the direction of the existing socio-political and economic order directly pushes, and encourage every kind of inequalities in society. Except a rigorous series of taxation methods, there exists no known means to curtail the evil of inequality.

The above mentioned method of ending the existing inequality regime would simply make sense on the following grounds:

a) When the unique avenues of expressing one's wealth no more exist, the proverbial greed to accumulate wealth should naturally get reduced. Greed is a result of the basic fear about future deprivations. When basic human dignity and freedom is protected and guaranteed, the mad urge to safe-guard it against future uncertainties would logically come to an end.

b) Consider that the total wealth of a nation is a corpus fund. When maximum of this fund is spent on constructing gigantic structures for the chosen elites, (say, 1%) or allowed to be kept by them in their private coffers, naturally, only the rest of the fund is available for meeting the life-needs of the remaining 99% common citizens ! When the community owned state resources are no more spent on select few elites and their lives, such hugely saved funds can now be used for building-up equal standard life-amenities for the entire population, as in the example of tube-rail service given above.

What the future of the world requires is a new model of progress, neither right, not left. A straight path in the middle is quite feasible, with an altered outlook on life, and towards fellow-beings, as shown in the blog link given above (http://newphilosophyoflife.blogspot.in/)

Article-11

Narration: In the above 9 articles, we have attempted to describe the various negative features, and logical and ideological inconsistencies of modern democracy with its implied values and meaning. Now, in this last article, we make an attempt to describe what an ideal democracy should be, and what it should represent to people and mankind.

What should a true democracy represent to people ?
(OR) A new theory of democratic society

There is utter confusion in the contemporary world as to what the democratic establishments must represent to the people ! What is the philosophical and metaphysical role of a human establishments that control the lives of people ? What is the real nature of relation between man and the modern state ?

In the old world such a question was not relevant as the ruler was there in every society as part of life, like the ever-present sky above ! Individual man was never a chooser here. He was a mere victim, the subject. But in the modern world, a clear definition is essential as man is supposed to be a free-entity unlike in the past, and the contemporary political system is known as 'democracy', an open system of 'equal men'.

Other than blind speculative theories and myths based on old traditions, no scientific light is there on this very tricky issue. But various kinds of governmental establishments thrive in the world, domesticating individuals, under the strength of various ideologies, theories and norms, many of them falsely clinging on to slogans on man's liberty, justice and equality ! But primarily all of them are there in the field for the benefit of their own unbridled personal freedom, making the establishment a legitimate and convenient means for their cunning intentions.

Are such establishments, especially those who claim themselves as democratic:

=> run on the collective will of the people ? If yes, what is it, and how accurately we could know and quantify it ?

=> are they based on the will of the majority ? If yes, won't it be against the basic principles of universalism ?

=>Do they exist to safe-guard the sovereignty and pride of a people ?

=> In our enlightened age of 'universalism', does the establishment genuinely strive to achieve tenets of world peace, universal brotherhood, and share mind and material with the co-existent ?

=>Or, are they plainly running an old model of authoritarian establishment on the pretext of being peoples' representatives ?

As most of the nations in the contemporary world claim to be DEMOCRATIC, irrespective of whether the man on the throne a self proclaimed king, a tyrant, or a military leader, we better concentrate our study on what should constitute a democracy where the throne is occupied by men from the species of 'people', after the formal ceremony of elections.

In a recent international Congress on 'Democratic culture' held at Olympia, Greece,(June 2012) there were as many number of notions on what democracy was, as the number of delegates from across the world ! There was no unanimity on what DEMOCRACY is, and what it should be.

Here the reason for even the worst of authoritarian regimes in contemporary world calling themselves DEMOCRACY is amply clear ! Democracy today merely means, the rule by some one from the people's class, irrespective of what he does under their rule, or the values he keep on human dignity and freedom, progress of mankind etc. Is it not the worst of calamities that could happen to mankind, as the realm of polity is what defines and determine not only the life of individual citizens, but also that of the entire nation, and through the collective element of nations, the very fate of human kind !

This paper attempts to arrive at some universal principles on Democracy, or for that reason, for any modern political establishment, to represent the **collective realm** of reason and common sense of people. It attempts to locate a distinct and clear realm of the 'collective' in the sense of reason of man that is ever alive and functioning, over and above the instincts of pure 'liberalism'. This paper attempts to show that, man has a distinct realm that is alive, and operate over and above his classical realm of self-interest, and often over the irrational whims of the self.

Existing theories on the origin of establishment in human societies

One of the lead theories is that of Thomas Hobbes and Sigmund Freud; that of the social contract. Man, out of his sense of reason, opted to constitute a collective institution of power to mange the problems that arise out of his collective living. While Hobbes described human nature as nasty and brutish in a state of nature, thus needing a collective power center to counter these trends, Freud's theory was also similar in theme and content. Freud said, the primordial brothers had to kill their father, the symbol of authority in their lives to liberate themselves. But the anarchy that followed after the killing had drowned them in remorse, and they had to decided to constitute a power center to discipline themselves, and to ward of anarchy in future !

Rousseau's theory was just opposite. He stated that the origin of the ancient forms of establishment and civil society was an act of extreme cunning-ness and selfishness from the part of the rich and powerful in the society, in the state of nature:

' the rich man, thus urged by necessity, (of protecting his vast property and other assets from the attack of the less privileged) conceived at length the profoundest plan that ever entered the mind of man: this was to employ in his favour the forces of those who attacked him, to make allies of his adversaries, to inspire them with different maxims, and to give them other institutions as favourable to himself as the law of nature was unfavourable' .... " Let us join", said he, " to guard the weak from oppression, to restrain the ambitious, and secure to every man the possession of what belonged to him: let us institute rules of justice and peace, to which all without exception may be obliged to conform"

The theory this author had proposed during early 1990s was similar to that of Rousseau in essence. It stresses more on the unholy nexus between the strongest to form the establishment,to keep off the ones who questions authority. It can be viewed at blog:http://originofestablishment.blogspot.in/

In Hobbes theory, the role of the sense of reason of man is at the forefront. In the other theories, the natural self-centeredness of man was the driving force in the setting up of the collective establishment. He wanted to use it for his own betterment than that of the society at large.

Whatever may be the speculative stories of the past that we might attribute as cause of the origin of our modern kind of establishment, it is a fact that the fate of our poor and the unprivileged in the world is at the mercy of the rich and the powerful, despite all our rhetoric on RIGHTS, JUSTICE and EQUALITY ! Irrespective of the kind of the establishment we have today in the contemporary world, above calamity is an un-challengeable reality. **Hence, there is a vital need for digging out better fundamentals from history, or from a better study of human nature and establish new theories that would** provide new platform to base our modern democratic institutions on a more noble and universally acceptable footing ! What should a collective institution of human society must represent to the people ?

No doubt, the task is not easy as what we are trying to arrive at is a theory of human society, and its institution of politics. Let us start the task with all hopes and a positive mind !

The liberal traditions of the old world was more profound, though on a different footing !

In a way, as Rousseau had thought, the man in a state of nature before the establishment of civil society was more liberated in many senses ! If one had adequate physical strength for himself, and if not, by assembling the strength of other like minded people, he could dethrone the worst of enemies of freedom by a direct coup. **As true even today, no law is strong enough to stop a man with real physical strength !** It was only a matter of free choice for any one, whether to abide under the rule of the strongest, or to rebel and try to out-throw him. The only difference today is the wide-spread sense of civility, that advocates for the advantages of living under a common law.

In those past days of wild freedom, every one had the freedom to borrow from a lender, and in case of failure to repay, to opt to be a slave or a servant, submitted to the lender ! In some way, no one could disagree that this kind of freedom, even to forfeit one's own 'self-hood' before another person, had greater profoundness than today's non-freedom even to attempt suicide,(the right to take away one's own life !) or to offer oneself as a slave to the other for favours, or material values received ! In fact we would be compelled to believe that the origin of slavery in the world was out of such perverted sense of freedom prevailed in the old world. Hence, it was considered so natural in the old world not to offer them right to vote etc, as slaves were entities who had surrendered their self-hood to someone else !

Right to kill each other in one to one duels was a routine affair in old European countries, as way of settling disputes ! With pistols, or swords in the hand, two men stand back to back, take a certain number of steps in opposite direction, and whoso-ever succeed in suddenly turn and injure/kill the other, used to be the winner in disputes ! How can we say that man did not enjoy freedom in those old societies ? It was freedom of an absolute kind, but very different from our definition of it in our contemporary world.

The instance of man's reason growing above his-own natural (animal) traits

The point this portion attempts to highlight is that a sense of universal justice and fairness had emerged in human mind that overruled the above crude sense of freedom and justice subjective to particular stages in history ! The Magna-Charta treaty, the American bill of the 'rights of man', and the French revolutionists' 'declaration of the rights of man, Lincoln's act of banning slave trade etc. were distinct and clear examples of this emergence of a new sense of justice and freedom of man, in the maturity of time in human history !

Witch hunting was banned in certain European countries, and child marriage and 'sati' (practice of brides killing themselves by jumping into the funeral-fire of their husbands in the Hindu societies of India) were also prohibited under law in countries like India.

 Man's **collective sense of reason (or mode of reason ?)** had emerged as something distinct, and overriding that of the individual sense of reason ! Man has shown that he has a distinct dimension in him that could act as the spirit, or a distinct entity representing the 'collective' reason within him. **He was able to express himself as a non-individual entity at times, exclusively representing his collectivism, or the social dimension of him**. Man exhibited his ability to express himself as a distinct collective 'spirit', a 'parallel self' within that exists alongside his individual-ego.

Man became able to foresee consequences of his own unrestrained individual acts turning harmful to his own disadvantage in the long run. Such vision and imagination was what prompted the old hunter-gatherer man to settle down near river beds, with an agrarian way of life.

He could see the inevitability of forming formal social set-up and institutions for leading a life of perpetual peace. This understanding has to be recognized as part of his inherent urge for keeping his body and environment clean and orderly.

He was able to realize that one's own freedom would be an intangible mirage without formalizing it for everyone in a legitimate social institutionalizing.

Of course such vision and imagination might not have emerged in every member of the group in one fine morning ! It might have emerged in the mind of a single man first, and he might have been able to share it with few others in his close circle. This phenomenon is true with every human achievement, and ideological progress in every human saga.

In the case of some men suddenly rising-up above his usual self, and thinking and acting on behalf of the society at large, we have no way but to accept this phenomenon as a ploy of NATURE for the development of human society in Her desired way !

Werner Krieglstein (college of Du Page, USA) in his paper titled 'The aesthetic dimension of democratic culture, and the wisdom of the crowds' (published in the Journal of International society for universal dialogue-9th Congress proceedings, Vol- 2) quotes Jonathan Haidt:

' According to Haidt, the creation of 'super organisms' is nature's way to solve the evolutionary problem of 'free-riders'. Free-riders are maladapted members of a group that do not contribute to the benefit and well-being of the community.'

Here the author support the idea of the collective reason of men at work in nature, to meet Her evolutionary needs. We have ample evidence in-front of us for this evolutionary pattern of human civilization so far; it was a sure and certain journey from more and more exclusivity and intolerance to more and more inclusiveness, tolerance and freedom, despite events such as the world wars, the holocaust, colonialism, and many atrocities of the tyrants in history ! It was an upward journey, without any doubt.

If man's body has its instincts intact to ensure its self-protection and growth needs, the mind also might be having its own instinctive system to look after man's spiritual self-protection, as well as its destined development. Man's irrepressible sense of freedom and justice needs no explanation and evidence, as there are innumerable stories and examples in history. The American revolution, followed by the French revolution, and then the many up-rising of the colonies against European rule are undeniable examples and evidence of this fierce sense of freedom and justice in the inners of man !

When the physique of man had transformed the thick jungles into towns and cities, made roads, railways and airports, the mind of man was also engaged in transforming its realm into more habitable avenues. The top most among it was his political realm- the realm of his collective. Just like his earnest interest and concern in his physical environment, he was equally keen about transforming his collective realm of living too. What a good physical environment does for the body, a healthy collective environment would do for this mind too. Hence, man's aspiration for a healthy political environment should be attributed to his inherent urge for ORDER, BEAUTY and BALANCE. We have no other option but to believe that what led man to build up bridges, roads and railways was at par with what led him to invent better political institutions for his collective living. Both the aspirations had a single source: his sense of REASON.

Of course there was a conflict: the conflict between those who wanted to stick on to the old ways, and those who aspired to embrace the new and the progressive. As Heraclitus had believed, conflict was essential in human society for its emerging into newer forms.

Here, we have clearly a sect of men those who want to stick on to their animal ways of self-interest, and self-centeredness, and the another sect, who want to go after the inherent, progressive urges of the mind and reason. As we have seen earlier, so far the victory was always with the later sect. Otherwise the human

civilization would not have progressed at all from its
jungle dimensions !

The need of the hour is to recognize and accept the inherent
urges, or instincts of every one's sense of reason to go on
progressing for ever. Such progress is distinctly and clearly a
walking away from his old jungle values and priorities ! Without
doubt, civilizational progress is a sure journey from man's
inherent animal nature, though it is known wrongly around his
better dwelling units, roads, number of high-end cities, and
other improved life- style amenities.

These inherent urges, or instincts of man's reason, beyond its
'order' and consistency sensing function must be recognized and
accepted by the modern age. What was that urged man to go
after his scientific, philosophic and spiritual pursuits that
ultimately has led to his civilizational development ? **The
Darwinian reproductive and growth instincts alone will not
have resulted in such phenomenal development of the brute
in the jungle to a civilized man of today.**

It has to be accepted by modern man, or at least he must
seriously probe into the hidden urges in him that led to his
civilizational growth. The pattern of development of man into
multitude of fields other than better food production can not be
blindly attributed to the 'competitive' instincts, again an aspect
of Darwinian evolutionary theory. His urge to invent and build-
up better collective socio-political institutions must go beyond
the competitive urge, and the struggle for survival. Here, man
clearly came out from his shell of SELFISHNESS, and attempted
to weave out social systems where he hoped collective living of
masses in mutual peace world be possible.

Every individual is born with a unique gene-equation, born into
an equally unique social surrounding and make an equally
unique social relation with his fellow-beings around. In every
respect, for nature, every unit of life appears to be unique, at
least that for human beings ! His spiritual tie with the Nature, or
the ultimate source of life is direct, and fully unique once again.
Hence, there is this distinct canvas where every man exists in a
different realm, the canvas of universe and the universal scheme

of things. The social canvas that man's collective institutions forcibly place him, with out the burden of accepting such uniqueness of every person, hence, indeed is an unnatural act. Our social institutions must have been tailor made to uphold and protect this uniqueness of every person, to be at par with the natural order concerning man's real spiritual identity.

Though in principle 'liberal' ideology stand for, and advocate this, in practical reality, our contemporary socio-political institutions just achieve the reverse; they end up forcibly placing every individual in the most impersonal web of a society and a country. Nations in-turn are the new unique entities, attempting to claim the unique status as once claimed by individuals in the beginning. In the clamor of nations for superiority over the other, real individuals are pushed back into the status of mere material and commodities for the making of nations and countries. Here individuals rot, while the unnatural collective entities thrive. This scheme of things shut off the individual from the original spiritual sources of nature, and make him a synthetic monster of sorts.

It is an empirical fact that only individuals could experience emotions and feelings; NOT any collective entity like communities, or nations. Hence, every collective institution must aim, and gets translated into effective 'means' for making the individuals experience life in better ways. Making institutions for its own sake does not make sense. In the contemporary world, the phenomenon of having institutions for its own sake, ignoring its individuals, is rampant. Institutions like politics, media and education transform individuals into VIRTUAL creatures that exist just to constitute and make the institutions ! This should be a very disturbing development, deserving serious attention of social scientists.

Tyrants and megalomaniac rulers utilize this phenomenon, and often wage damaging wars and conquers, by getting large masses converted effectively into such virtual creatures ! Hitler's such acts are in front of the modern age as best example of this danger.

The hidden directives within

It is beyond doubt that there is an internal urge within man that always seek 'order' and consistency in what ever he does, and also in his surroundings. It is this mysterious urge that made man to seek out and establish better 'collective' systems. (social and political systems)

But this mysterious and positive urges work only when man enjoys FREEDOM in society, wherein he could exercise his sense of reason without bounds !When this free exercise of individual freedom is restricted beyond a limit, he always shows negative tendencies of destruction of his own self, that of others around, and also his surroundings. This negative trend that any one of us could experience within in the real life situations, could be nature's native strategy to 'destroy and rebuild'. To restore order from the chaos around, the existing system, or the cause of disorder must be destroyed first, so that a new order could arise. This is a convincing argument to support negative behaviors of individual man, and also that of larger societies who suffer, or might have suffered atrocities and brutal violations of their rights and freedom from the hands of oppressors, and oppressive regimes !

The lesson hence to be learned that, those who device socio-political systems must ensure that, such system does not cause violation of any one's freedom and rights !

We must believe that the above mentioned mysterious inherent urge for 'ORDER' within man might have been the reason behind his scientific and philosophic aspirations.

We must observe elements above and beyond animal instincts here. Man has started seeing himself in future. This futuristic vision was that had marked him clearly above the animal nature. He started having reverence for his own life, and the 'existence' as a whole.

We shall see how this 'reverence' for self, and life in general had helped him to visualize his 'sacred realms of the collective', in the next part of this study.

The root fundamental element behind the emergence of concepts like FREEDOM, JUSTICE etc was a REVERENCE for life !

Just like the never ending debates around the origin of establishment in human communities, list of theories is also long about the origin of the wonder concepts like LIBERTY, FREEDOM, EQUALITY, JUSTICE and DEMOCRACY in the world ! Theories run on arguments like victory of man's sense of reason, the physical victory of the parties seeking freedom over their oppressors and suppressors etc.etc. Though Magna Charta treaty of 13th century AD is considered as the first distinct event in modern history where concept of FREEDOM was first emerged, a less popular story some hundred years prior - that in AD-1100- the 'charter of liberties' consented by King Henry 1 is also there in record. King Henry faced displeasure from the powerful Church and the popes, as well as from the powerful barons upon his accession to the throne. He consented to restrict his own arbitrary traditional powers by issuing **'a charter of liberties'** to the later group, again succumbing to the pressure from the freedom seekers !

In Magna Charta treaty also, the Nobles had to raise a force against the King to make him succumb. He was made to sign the treaty restraining his powers for arbitrary confiscation of ships and other properties of the former, arrest with out proper trials etc. Freedom was sought and obtained. Freedom was something demanded at gun point and forcibly obtained !We can argue that there is nothing like 'freedom' naturally existing in nature, but it was 'invented' by the Nobles for their own personal benefit !

But the story of FREEDOM like concepts got a shocking twist during the American revolution. The revolutionists evoked ' the self evident' nature of Freedom for man ! We can not rest the necessity of freedom on any well acceptable syllogism. Syllogism depends on linking a current argument on some universally accepted prior principles or established truth. Here concepts like 'freedom' had no precedent in human history, hence, first time in history, it was declared self-evident. (We can not ignore a similar evoking of the 'universal sense of what is right' about the

5th century democracy in Athens, by historian Thucydides, during King Pericles' funeral address !)

Here we squarely land up at the door of human reason. Man has no other known faculty that could give sudden birth to such wonder concepts like Freedom and justice. Freedom like concepts can not be objects of our external senses like eyes, or ears, hence, such 'universal sense', or self evident 'feeling' can not be an object of anything other than our sense of reason !

As our current knowledge about faculty of reason is not much advanced, we do not know how it could originate such wonder concepts from time to time. But we have no other alternative. Every one of us distinctly and clearly feel the need of freedom, liberty, justice and democracy within. It is a universal feeling. Hence it is self evident. It is like LOVE. Love can not be seen or heard or touched. We all are able to feel its devastating sway within, at some or other point of our lives !

(A recent book titled ' Is reason a sense organ? ' (Amazon.com) argues that human reason indeed is a sense organ yet to be recognized by man, and why we are able to sense feelings like love and freedom is due to its 'sense organ status !)

Contemporary writers like Charles Taylor (Duke University) in his popular study titled ' On Social imaginary' points towards the emergence of a MORAL ORDER in the world, thanks to its origin in the minds of certain creative individuals/thinkers first, and then spreads as a prominent idea into the mainstream.

" **My basic hypothesis is that central to Western modernity is a new conception of the**moral order of society. **This was at first just an** "idea" **in the minds of some influential thinkers, but it later came to shape the social imaginary of large strata, and then eventually whole societies. It has now become so self-evident to us,** that we have trouble seeing it as one possible conception among others"

He is not specific as to its source of origin. How was the idea of 'moral order' emerges in the minds of creative people virtually from no where ? Unless some tangible explanation is offered, such origin of ideas would equal to fiction, or pure speculation. It is high time that man realizes the role of the sense (organ) of reason in the emergence of such concepts and ideas into the human society, through the minds of some creative people.

Ideas and concepts can not spread in the world in the form of thought particles through a storm like, physical event. Hence, the only route of it would be through selected creative minds.

When man considers the existence of hundreds of human glands that produces known and not yet known excretions into the body system, for known and unknown purposes, emergence of such periodical ideas and concepts into the 'collective realm' of the world for its mystery development should be quite acceptable to human reason ! These ideas and concepts played central role in transforming human society and its polity beyond words ! Hence, we should not shy away from accepting the source of these concepts, such as freedom, justice, human dignity and democracy, as the mystery sense (organ) of reason !

Here, this writer attempt to convey that, all the above concepts, or ideas must have originated from a single unifying property of human development, that is the development of a certain REVERENCE FOR LIFE in the human mind.

The primitive hunter became a 'gatherer' in the ladder of this development first. Gathering involved an acceptance of future, an awareness of time. Life was accepted as an ongoing process. Gatherer has transformed into a cultivator of land; a settler. Man could identify himself as a separate entity from the LIFE process. It was a division with great relevance. As we have learned from science, knowing more involves dividing wholes into parts. Man seemed realized that he is a traveler of a sort in the vehicle of life ! He started burial of dead bodies. This could be the beginning of his crude spirituality, and hence, the emergence of REVERENCE for life, and person hood !

This was the clear departure of man from his animal stage ! His 'reason' was made to carry him miles and miles away from the pure material realm of the existence of animals. His reason can not ever be defined and explained on the usual lines of apparatus to find intelligent means to meet his material ends, or a historical, or cultural by-product that is purely mechanical to lead him to smarter survival, with more efficient competition techniques to out-smart the opposition. It is a self-evident fact that, man's special 'reason' has lead him to unimaginably strange realms of progress, which can not be explained on biological paradigm alone.

It is more sensible here to attribute this sense of REVERENCE for life as trigger for the origin of religions in human history than attributing its cause to primordial fear about the uncertainties of life ! We have already seen that, natural emergence of ideas, concepts and notions though the route of Reason is a routine norm of human existence. Insisting for the opposite view is a reluctance to come out from the animal mentality of the primordial times.

Apart from the cold biological reasoning based on ends and means, for that even animals are known to exhibit reasoning faculty pretty well, (Capuchin monkeys are famous for keeping specially kept stone-hammers and stone slabs for breaking hard shelled nuts, and even rolling down heavy stones from hill top to scare away predator Leopards !) man always exhibited several behaviors un-explainable by the said of logic of biological ends and means - -say, his art and craft from time immemorial, his talent for creating and enjoying music, his fierce sense of freedom and self-pride, his longing for justice and fair-play in deals etc.etc. are traits beyond the usual biological explanation.

The hunter-gatherer has turned more a thinker-doer ! The mind started gaining more relevance in human life than physical body, and its animal, or biological instincts. Man started to perceive a higher entity within, beyond the body.

Nature seems to have bestowed different kinds of 'reason organ' to different species, depending upon their pre-ordained destinies. Each reason unfolds to its fullest potentials as the species grow by. With man, his reason and destiny was very, very special, as his story of unprecedented development has already witnessed ! There are many more higher steps lurking in his future, judging from its past history.

This newly emerged sense of REVERENCE about his person, and life in general, must have given birth for ancillary concepts like FREEDOM, LIBERTY, JUSTICE and DEMOCRACY. This proposition is more sensible to believe than the emergence of different concepts like 'moral order' or concept of 'Freedom' and justice in human society at different periods of time. Concluding on the more fundamental sense of reverence would be like arriving at a 'unifying' theory on physics !

Stories of many ancient kings restoring the defeated kingdoms to its own owner, and pardoning and leaving the defeated opponent to his own fate are many in history. Kings often married from the family of the surrendered opponent, and continued life journey in positive spirit. Journey of human civilization was one from rigid exclusivity to more and more openness and inclusiveness, with out any doubt.

Shape of the 'public imagery', or the 'public sphere' , or the 'realm of the collective'

During the time of the rule by kings, feudal Lords, or the foreign invaders, the 'public realm' was out of bound for ordinary people. Its shape and form was the exclusive areas of the strong man who wore the crown to decide.

Only after the end of Kingdoms and its likes, and during the emergence of democratic ideas that the question of its shape, values and form had arisen. The end purpose of this reflection is to propose to the men of mind in the world that, as every citizen has an inherent conception of what a 'public sphere' must be, based on his inherent sense of REVERENCE for life and his person-hood, the time for its multiple interpretations based on the power holder's rhetoric prowess should end !

In a recently concluded 'international congress for universal dialogue' at Olympia, Greece,(this conference was also referred to once in the beginning of this paper) where a hundred philosophers and thinkers from across the globe had participated, and the chief theme 'democratic culture: historic reflections and modern transformations' was discussed, and papers presented. Participants were wonder stuck upon hearing such varied interpretations of the base democratic idea ! While the Chinese and many of the African nations argued for a community based person hood, and a democracy fit for such a democracy where the community level heads take decisions and maintain public conduct, European and US delegates staunchly protected a democracy based on the supreme rights of the single individual ! Russians appeared a confused lot, as they could never taste any true form of democracy.

The atmosphere was in tune with the post-modern PLURALISTIC world view. World has no final truth, or definition in hand about anything, including for concepts like democracy and freedom. So, it is better we carry on with the world as it is, with all its definitions of truths and non-truths, constantly engaging in helpful dialogues !

It is equal to pure chaos, but beautifully packed in words like 'pluralism' and 'multiculturalism' ! There are groups and classes in the contemporary world who do not mind the world going this way. Rather they find clear advantages in its going this way. People will be unbound plain 'consumers' of multitudes of industrial products, uninhibited by any ideological, moral, or religious principles. They will compete each other, kill each other, for being loyal to such a system. Being loyal pays in such systems. Loyalty is anti-freedom. Those who want only the goodies of such lives will not ever cry for individual freedom. They will seek only the left over from the tables of the rich and the mighty, which they are too willingly oblige. Hence, the current system has all the support accessories to go on for ever successfully !

But the thinking minority, those who care for future of every one's coming generations realize that the ' public realm' has never lost its original purity' and clarity of concept. It was always the ultimate embodiment of man's clearest of wisdom, reason, and common sense - -**man always wished that the realm of the collective should always be above partisan whims and wishes, but a pure realm of all that is sensible, wise and rational, that would ensure justice, freedom, liberty and happiness for all !**

Concepts and imagery of the SACRED REALM OF THE COLLECTIVE are universal in nature ! No one belongs to humanity would ever raise objections to such an imagery, or the realm of collective as a distinct conception. It is based on the nature-bestowed sense of reason of man, and the good judgment of every human being. He fully realizes that if he seek only his own, or his group's selfish interest and victory always, and ignore and discard the interests of others, it won't be a sustainable proposition, or idea. Hence, only those who with short vision, or with limited sense of rationality would insist for the opposite ! Without doubt, those who are not interested in lasting solutions for the collective problems of mankind would insist for the opposite conceptions of the collective.

For the self-image and self-identity, an appropriate canvas of the collective is an existential necessity

We have already seen the role of the collective myths about the 'public sphere', in shaping the egos of the individual members in society. Often individuals are helplessly draw heavily from the 'imagery' of the collective to draw the picture of his own self. This is true with the way any object in the world gains its identity; identity of every object is gained in relation with other objects around in space and time. Man can not identity anything without relating to some thing else. Here in the case of man, he needs a public canvas to place his self into. This canvas is often chosen subjectively for various identities one keep, but a canvas such as a state is always imposed upon in the old world. In the modern world, such a canvas must be and could be kept sacred and reverend, so that individuals could gains their healthy identities and self-image.

After all, civilization was solely a matter of widening this canvas of the 'collective' of man; the animal that he, was living in the pit of his selfish nature. When the CATEGORY of society, or collectivity entered in his sense of reason in the maturity of time, he could elevate himself from the said pit of animal nature to the identity of a civil being. It was only a matter of altering the canvas. Today, we say ours' is a globalized world. It simply means the canvas the self of man resides has been extended larger and wider. It is purely a conceptual exercise, a matter of mind, and it is this exceptional ability of man to build-up his self on concepts and ideas that made him different from animals. He has two distinct selves, one a purely biological one that shares with animals, and the other his notional self (ego) that resides in a world of concepts and ideas.

Above explained facts, which are nothing but empirical, reiterates the extreme relevance of keeping the **realm of the collective** as sacred, sane, and healthy !

The existential as well the political need of keeping man's realm of collective sacred and pure is well evident, and self-evident.

With out doubt, the chief character of man's 'realm of collective' should be built around the sense of REVERENCE, as we have seen its foundational nature for every aspect of human civilization. This sense of reverence was what had given birth to the concept of INDIVIDUAL DIGNITY in human societies. Freedom, justice, and equality all are mere necessary features of men with individual dignity. Men, in the state of nature, ie. in the absence of any organized 'collective' establishment, tend to be 'nasty and brutish', as only such an attitude would ensure his safety and survival. Even when the 'collective' act in a predatory manner, with out caring to exhibit its mandatory 'SACRED' nature, man will revert to his 'nastiness and brutishness', as we often see under many States in the world. When his self is under threat, civilized man tend to go back to his basic animal nature.

This sacred realm has another CENTRAL dimension too; that as **the IDEAL 'OTHER'**.It is the other who makes or breaks the world for every human being. One's self is nothing but his 'armor', or 'pattern of reaction' towards others around him. **The concept of peoples STATE (democratic establishments) was basically devised to make each citizen behaving in a civilized manner with the other person, and towards the very concept of their SACRED COLLECTIVE-NESS.** Hence, modern democratic establishments could be modeled as the IDEAL OTHER, for its much required PRINCIPLED functioning. As we have discussed above at many places, the absence of any imitable model of peoples own government was the chief draw back of democracy, when the reins were landed in their hands from the older authoritarian regimes. Hence, this new MODEL could be developed into practical aspects of our modern democratic governments.

While accepting the highly civilized status of our modern world by one and all, including political leaders and industry heads, they can not discard the above principles of its base foundation.

What our existing realm of collective represents to people ?

The difference between what is in paper, and what is real is stark evident today. What is in paper is every democratic nation's CONSTITUTION document. It has many elements of above seen SACREDNESS, with a beautiful mission and vision statement, such as the very motto of the state is to provide equality, fraternity and liberty to each its individual member etc.etc. But in practice, our modern day democratic institutions are open fields of war among political groups to grab the proverbial seats of governmental authority !

The great art and science of POLITICS has replaced the realm of collective altogether. It is nothing but a grouping of the strongest and the smartest to run the realm of collective, for the limitless opportunities it offers to enjoy the traditional fruits of POWER and POLITICAL authority. Though such forms of democratic political institutions was exclusively meant to protect the weak from the strong, it has unfortunately turned an institutionalized scheme of things wherein the strong continue to have upper hand in the society, and the avenues of the weak even to protest rights violations has been taken away from him in the name of keeping tendencies of SEDITION checked, and at times, even in the name of plain patriotism !

If we say that these modern day political establishments represent the primeval FEAR and ANTAGONISM against the stranger-outsider-OTHER to own community, it would be an appropriate description to understand their attitude towards its citizens ! In those primeval jungle days, every tribal community used to treat any outsider as an enemy and a threat. Hence, these enemies were always used to be caught, tied and brought before the community assembly, and often tortured and killed in a ritualistic manner. When observed closely at our modern political establishments , their police and mass media system, criminals and offenders of any sort are always treated the way those old primeval communities used to treat their stranger-outsiders ! The prime emotions in play here too is, it should be believed, the old fear and antagonism towards the stranger-other. One who committed a crime, or an offense suddenly turns an outsider to the community. Here modern societies ignore all their civic norms, and fall straight into their primeval mind-set.

At some unfortunate turn in the history, the democratic institutions did not care, or had not taken adequate notice of the utter need of reforming the old power and authority oriented governmental forms of the past to suit the special needs of a government of EQUAL CITIZENS. Hence, those old forms of authoritarian establishments, along with all its old myths of princely wealth of the state, police, taxation laws, courts and jails had passed over, as it was, to manage the 'ruling' aspect of the government of equal citizens too !

All the mythological, and fatal attractions of old KINGDOMS had crept into democratic form of government too ! Hence, the SACRED REALM OF COLLECTIVE has transformed into a fierce field of fight for the crown. Democracy has become a legitimate fight for grabbing these much desired seats of power by professional groups specialized in the filed.

The peoples class is mere passive material for the existence and running of modern political regimes. The Kings of the olden days, though used to treat the kingdom and its people as an extension of his own self, being the sole authority of such Kingdoms he used to have some sort of natural affinity towards whatever remain under his authority and ownership. But under modern day democratic-political establishments, with its fierce impersonal structure of government and its authority, and thanks to its highly hierarchical model, such natural empathy and care towards the COUNTRY or its inhabitants is totally lacking ! This orphaned state of the people at large in the world is a unique state of affairs in history !

Hence, the sacredness in the paper, and the practical reality of modern day politics have turned into two opposite poles. No amount of rational or moral persuasion from any quarter seems effective to cure this problem, as the former class had already taken over the reigns of 'power and authority', mythologically associated with those seats. Hence, nations and the world at large is under siege of a sort these days. The traditional 'peoples voice'- the media- has opted to stand neutral, as they are mostly owned and run by the industry, with whose active partnership such modern day democratic institutions operate and run.

Thomas Hobbes had described human nature as 'nasty and brutish', that made the existence of collective realm of men absolutely necessary in human societies. But today, these collective realms that have been instituted as remedy, are that turned 'nasty, brutish and dark' , to the utter bewilderment of human race ! Such realms at the center of our life gives very damaging examples to our younger generation. **Society as a whole learn their basic lessons of life from the dynamics of this realm.** In all sense, modern world is living with a great self-deception with its political realm, especially with regard its democratic institutions.

The greatest task before our age is to get these realms transformed into realms of ' reverence' for life and human dignity. Some way out has to be found as to how to turn these realms into centers of human reason, wisdom and common sense.

Global institutions like UN and its multiple wings, unfortunately, are not found different in their stand and operations from that of typical governmental bodies, though they were set-up with much hope for mankind. Such institutions also must introspect how genuinely and effectively they represent the 'sacred realm of collective'of mankind.

The conflict between 'liberalism' and democratic notions

To some modern thinkers, there is a marked conflict between liberalism and democracy, as liberalism stands for unbound individual freedom, whereas democracy demands great amount of tolerance towards the fellow-citizens, especially in the modern multicultural world.

Anayra Santory, in the paper titled ' The democratic exit for liberalism' (Journal of the International Society for Universal Dialogie-Vol-111, page 351) states that: 'The liberal philosopher, although believing he can justify liberalism and its basic virtues, is in effect, just sweeping under the rug of the private all which he is not willing to discuss because his lack of commitment to democracy'

We have seen in the beginning of this paper that the freedom of man in the old world was more profound in principle that of today, but it was dangerous and not sustainable in the long run. We have seen how a 'sense of reason' over and above the individual reason and selfishness had arrived in the midst of human society in the maturity of time, as if in a natural evolutionary course. When the perennial fear of the other person could be gradually removed by rational human political institutions, man would fearlessly allow the other person to have his ways, thus receiving in return, his own unbound freedom too ! Such a stage in society is still a mirage, and a utopia because, our so called democratic political institutions were not successful in restoring the confidence of the individual citizens about his unbound freedom in modern states ! We have seen the reasons behind this calamity in clear terms above.

Conclusion : The mutated societies and its members, ie. the people

We have seen above how real is the habitat of the mind in the modern world. If bodies mutate in the act of being adapted to the physical environment as the evolutionary laws say, the mind of man also should mutate to adapt to the needs of his ' body' collective ! If the realm of collective often offers a very hostile environment, the Ego adapts to such hostile environment, by adopting a fittingly resistant type of personality, ie, being hostile and aggressive himself ! Such adaptive techniques are nothing but one's survival needs. Modern world is totally unaware of this phenomenon. It believes that man is his physical self only. The man of mind is still a fiction for our modern day collective institutions, as it gives it more freedom from its responsibilities to treat and consider human being with more dignity, esteem and sense of reverence. In mind-set, and base spirit, we have seen that our modern day democratic institutions are not different from that of the old authoritarian and political power oriented, 3rd party establishments.

This modern reality of the hostile and aggressive individuals talks a lot about the sad reality of our 'realm of collective'. This realm should have taken birth out of the active knowledge, and under the active/ live responsibility of enlightened societies, instead of leaving it at the mercy of professional political players, who act with selfish motives. Such abandoning of this important realm unguarded and un-cared for, like an orphaned property, is against man's universal sense of what is right and fair. It is equal to abandoning life, and our personal selves, into the hands of alien people, and to their unknown whims and fancies. It is equal to leaving the world ORPHANED, with out any guardian to look after it !

It is time that we, the people of this enlightened age wake- up the relevance of these subtle aspects of our life on the planet, and take the bridle in our hands, in order to be responsible to ourselves and to our future generations.

There is no confusion now as to what modern democracies should represent itself to its people. What they must represent is the 'sacred realm of collective' of the people, as described above in all details.

-----------------------------------end-----------------------------------

Part-1 of this Book is available in Printed, as well as KINDLE format now, at Amazon.com

Is modern democracy a fake coin? :
http://www.amazon.com/dp/B008NNPG32

93

www.ingramcontent.com/pod-product-compliance
Lightning Source LLC
Chambersburg PA
CBHW070801290526
45795CB00002B/590